Contents

Acknowledgements

We are grateful to the Longman Group UK Ltd., on behalf of the Literary Executor of the late Sir Ronald A Fisher, F.R.S. and Dr Frank Yates F.R.S. for permission to reproduce 'Critical values of chi squared' and 'Critical values of *t*'from *Statistical Tables for Biological, Agricultural and Medical Research* 6/e (1974). We also wish to thank Cambridge University Press, and Mrs Ruth Green and Dr Frances Clegg, for their kind permission to use 'Critical values of Pearson's r' and 'Critical values of the Binomial Sign Test' respectively. Acknowledgement should also be given to Harper Collins Publishers for 'Critical values in the Mann-Whitney U Test', and to McGraw-Hill Publishing Co. for 'Critical values of T in the Wilcoxon Signed Ranks test'.

Introduction

If, as some social scientists believe, research methods are evolving, then this book is offered, not as an effort to prevent the extinction of a lumbering dinosaur, no longer adapted for modern life, but as an attempt to discover something useful and use it to invigorate current research thinking through crossbreeding. Counselling is a meeting place for many disciplines and we wish to add an appreciation of statistical procedures to that mix.

We would like to make it clear that the data and situations used to illuminate the worked examples are all invented by us.

Damian would like to thank his wife, Eileen and daughter Ruth for motivation, inspiration and distraction in almost equal measure. He also thanks Simon Collet for graphic advice and The Tansads for providing the soundtrack.

Pete would like to thank Jake, Rosie, Hannah and Sam for putting up with his 'absence' and Maggie for calming the panics.

We would both like to thank Maggie Taylor-Sanders for typesetting the tables, proofreading and editing.

Pete Sanders and Damian Liptrot
Manchester 1994

We dedicate this book to

Liz Shaw

Without her teaching and support over many years, this book
would never have been written.

Mapping Out The Territory

"There are three kinds of lies: lies, damned lies and statistics."
Disraeli

Students of all 'applied' subjects from agriculture to zoology study statistics, and practitioners in all such applied subjects are told that they need a working knowledge of statistics and how statistics relates to the subject in question. Counselling and counsellors have, by and large, escaped from the dreaded statistics courses...until now, that is. In the past year or so there has been a flurry of interest in research amongst counsellors in the UK and along with it has come an interest, even if born only out of necessity, in statistics. Indeed, your authors are currently busy spreading rumours that the subject of statistics is 'sexy' and will definitely be the next 'Big Thing' in counselling.

The trouble is that many of us know the truth, i.e. that all students of applied subjects will not only have studied statistics, but will often wonder why, say it's irrelevant and wonder what on earth it's got to do with them. It seems as though statistics is cursed to be the subject that is universally dull and boring and only used by time-served members of The Department of Misinformation. It would be nice to think that after reading this book (or as much of it as you need) you will be able to answer these 'Why'?' and 'What's it got to do with counselling?' questions with new insight and some conviction that the subject of statistics is our tool, not we its slaves.

What are Inferential Statistics?
This book is about a certain type of statistics used in social science research called inferential statistics. Statistics can be 'descriptive', 'inferential' or 'correlational'. Having conducted a study, and

obtained some results, it is likely that you will want to know what the results tell you about the behaviour of your subjects. You will probably want to subject them to some type of statistical analysis. You are faced with the choice of what type of statistical analysis you wish to perform on your data; descriptive, inferential or correlational.

1. Descriptive statistics are procedures which range from diagrams to simple calculations, which summarise or help to illustrate the data so that the main points can be grasped almost 'at a glance'. As their name suggests, the function of descriptive statistics is to describe the data you have obtained. When you collect your results you may have a large table full of figures (raw data). Simply looking at the table of results tells very little about what you have found. The raw data has to be treated in some way and the first type of treatment applied is usually a descriptive procedure.

In most investigations we do not test all the members of a particular population, but instead use a sample of that population. For example, we would not study all couples undergoing counselling with Relate, but take a sample and study them. When we have taken the sample we will probably want to use the sample to say something about the whole population. Descriptive statistics would not allow us to do this, they would simply describe the data that has been obtained from that particular group of subjects. We do not know if we would get the same pattern of results if we tested another group of subjects in the same way; so we do not know whether the results obtained from our sample represent what would happen in the rest of the population. We would use inferential statistics to do this.

2. Inferential statistics on the other hand, is a series of procedures, usually more complicated than the simple calculations used in descriptive statistics, whose purpose is to allow the user to *infer* something from the data. What is inferred is usually something about a cause and effect relationship or an association between variables.

* Why do statistical tests?
As mentioned above, when we conduct an investigation we

generally use a sample of the population as our subjects. But, what we want to use our results for is to say something about the likely behaviour of the whole of the population. We wish to use our results to make an inference about the population as a whole. Subjecting our results to analysis using the statistical tests in this book will allow us to make such inferences.

* What about probability and significance?
Inferential statistical procedures or tests revolve around the likelihood or *probability* that the results of research are due to chance. We employ the test to quantify the possible effects of chance then we compare our data to these figures. We then have to decide upon how far removed from these chance figures our results have to be before we are confident that they are due to our endeavours as researchers. This decision point is known as 'significance' see page 23.

When we conduct an inferential statistical test we are working out the likelihood (probability) that the results we obtained came from chance factors rather than what went on in the experiment (the manipulation of the independent variable). If having conducted the statistical test the difference between the sets of figures (or the relationship in the case of a correlation) is sufficiently large to be judged unlikely to be due to chance factors, we can reject the null hypothesis and accept the alternate hypothesis. We are confident that the results are due to the experimental procedures. More importantly, that were we to repeat the experiment (or correlation) on further samples of the population, we would obtain a similar pattern of results. In other words, what is true of our sample is likely to be true for the population as a whole. A significant effect, (difference or correlation) is one that is unlikely to have arisen due to chance.

* How do I know whether a difference is significant or not?
When you have conducted a statistical test on your results, you will end up with a single figure referred to as your **obtained value**. You then compare your obtained value with a figure referred to as the **critical value** (which will be found in the critical value tables at the back of the book). This comparison between your obtained

value and the critical value will tell you whether or not you can reject your null hypothesis.

3. Correlational statistics is a genuine third category where the size and type of *relationship* between two (or more) variables is measured. In this book, however, we will be treating correlational statistics as another form of inferential statistics. We think it makes sense because that is the way they are actually used in the real world. We would also point out that correlational procedures do not tell us anything about cause and effect relationships. This point is covered better in Sanders and Liptrot (1993) p116-122 see below.

Data for use in inferential statistical procedures is, in social sciences, gathered using *research methods* of one kind or another. Such methods often hinge upon taking a small sample of observations and then generalising these back to the population from which they were taken. Inferential statistics are concerned with the likelihood or probability that the results in the sample are due to some manipulation of events by the researcher and not due to chance factors alone.

If you are not familiar with quantitative research methods, cause and effect relationships or association between variables, types of data or descriptive statistical procedures, then you should read **An Incomplete Guide to Basic Research Methods and Data Collection for Counsellors** by Pete Sanders and Damian Liptrot (1993) PCCS.

Understanding how to Choose the Right Test

Much is made of choosing the correct statistical procedure. We have simplified the process as much as we think possible and we present simple decision-trees for you to follow in the Charts on pages 12 and 13 with more explanation on page 10. However, computer buffs have an acronym GIGO meaning 'garbage in - garbage out', which roughly describes what happens if you put inappropriate data into a statistical test. The decision regarding which test to use in any given situation is inextricably linked with an appreciation of the design of research methods. Also crucial to this decision is an understanding of the nature of types of data.

Our starting point for the present book is that you have read our previous book on research methods and data collection (Sanders and Liptrot 1993). If you are unfamiliar with any of the concepts in the present book as you go along, go back and read the above or a similar publication. Whatever statistical test is used, it will tell you whether any difference between the sets of scores is significant or not (unless you are performing a correlation, in which case it will tell you whether the relationship is significant or not). To some extent your choice of statistical test is limited by the design you have used in your investigation; there are certain statistical tests designed for specific types of design. However there is yet another choice; whether your statistical test is a parametric or a non-parametric test.

Parametric and Non-Parametric Tests
There are two categories of inferential statistical procedure covered in this book; parametric and non-parametric. They refer to the types of data that the test requires if it is to function correctly. (Like petrol and diesel engines, statistical tests require different types of 'fuel'.) There is, however, no short cut to using inferential statistical procedures without understanding the meaning of these and other terms and the differences between the two types. Your authors think that learning this is not only quite easy, but also since you've chosen to read this book, probably very useful too. Don't be put off by words like parametric and non parametric. In this case they do actually mean something and in general we believe that wherever you can show us a big word, we can show you a pretty simple concept. First we need to look at a couple of definitions. You should be familiar with the terms populations and samples. Whenever we measure a feature of a population (e.g. central tendency or variance) the measure is called a *population parameter*. If we measure a feature of a sample (again, let's say central tendency or variance) it's called a *sample statistic*.

  * **Parameters** are measures made of features of a population.
  * **Statistics** are measures made of features of a sample.

You should also know that the purpose of most research is to make guesses about (estimate) the features of a population (the population parameters) by measuring the features of samples (the sample statistics). See Sanders and Liptrot (1993) p70-76.

Parametric Tests are tests which base their calculation on an estimate of population parameters using sample statistics. Usually this involves the mean and standard deviation. (You can find the formulae for standard deviation buried in the workings of parametric tests in this book.) In order to use these population parameters fully, the test has to make certain assumptions about the data you are feeding into it (see page 7). Making these assumptions saves us a huge amount of laborious calculation. It also makes the tests more *powerful* and *efficient* than their non-parametric counterparts.

By '**powerful**' we mean that parametric tests have more power to detect a real or significant effect, assuming there is one to detect. It makes sense, then to choose a parametric test if it is possible to do so. Another way of putting this is to say that parametric tests are more sensitive. By '**efficient**' we mean that a parametric test will tell you that there is a significant effect when there really is one, using fewer measurements than an equivalent non-parametric test under the same circumstances. In some situations where subjects are difficult to obtain, this can be invaluable.

Both these advantages stem from the way in which parametric tests make use of the data obtained from your study. If you were to conduct both a parametric and non-parametric test on the same set of data you would soon notice some differences between the two. In non-parametric tests (such as a Wilcoxon test) what usually happens is that the test scores are converted into ranks and the calculation is then performed using this data. This always degrades the data or takes some of the information out of it. On the other hand, when using parametric tests, the whole of the calculation is conducted using the scores (with all their original richness of information) as they were obtained from the subjects.

At this point you may be thinking that if parametric tests are the more desirable, why not use them all the time? One way of looking at this question is to think of record players. Imagine you had an old style record player and a modern one. Whenever possible you would want to use your modern one, because it will make the records sound better. However, you may be asked to play your grandmother's old 78 rpm records. You cannot do this on your modern player because it will only play singles and LPs so you are forced to choose the old record player.

The assumptions of parametric tests.

1 : Interval or Ratio Data. The major characteristic of both interval and ratio data is that the distance between each point on the scale is equal. For example, one inch is exactly the same as any other inch, or a difference of 5 miles per hour is the same amount of speed whether the increase is from 20 to 25 mph or from 60 to 65 mph. In counselling research much of the data will not be interval or ratio. For example, is each point on a scale of self esteem identical to any other point, or does an increase in client satisfaction from 5 to 6 mean exactly the same increase in satisfaction if the change were from 8 to 9?

To decide whether data is suitable for parametric tests, use the 'B & Q test'. Think of what you are measuring - if you can buy something to measure it at B & Q, the chances are that it will be interval or ratio data. If you can't measure it using something from B & Q, you will probably have to use a non-parametric test. For example, if you are measuring time, you could buy a clock from B & Q to measure it, but if you were measuring self esteem or client satisfaction the probability is that B & Q does not stock something to measure it.
Note : The above example is intended to be a rule of thumb only, apply it in that sense and you won't go far wrong. The test is only referred to as the B & Q test because it is the nearest DIY store to my house. Should any other firms wish to sponsor the test, please contact me via the publisher. (Damian)

2: The data obtained are drawn from a normal distribution.

Whatever ability or behaviour is being measured should be normally distributed within the population. This is because most variables we might measure in counselling research are the product of a large number of variables acting at random (see Sanders and Liptrot 1993) p103-107. If you think about your data you should be able to work out if it falls into the above category. Should you really need to check for this you should either draw a histogram of the results, check the symmetry of the distribution by working out the mean median and mode or if you really want to go to town on your data, check them using a chi squared test for goodness of fit (page 41).

3: Equal Variance of the Two Sets of Data [Actually, this assumption is called 'Homogeneity of Variance' and to be absolutely accurate, it doesn't mean that the variances have to be equal. However, for the purposes of this book we've chosen to explain it as 'equal variance'.] Besides being drawn from a normal distribution, parametric tests make the assumption that the two sets of scores are equal in the degree of spread away from the mean. There are three ways of checking this:

1. Draw a frequency distribution (e.g. a histogram) of each set of scores and compare them.

2. Work out the mean and range for both sets of scores and compare them.

Note: Both these methods are 'rough and ready'. You can use them if the work you are doing is also rough and ready or when you're confident enough to know what you're doing.

3. Work out the variance of each set of scores and compare them using a procedure known as the F-ratio or F-test. It is a relatively simple procedure and is included in this book on page 95.

Note: You will only need to do an F-test if it's crucial that you're absolutely sure about your data.

4: Some tests are robust. If the data does not meet the requirements for a parametric test then you must use a non-parametric test. There are important exceptions to this rule, though: t-tests and one-way ANOVAs are what's known as **robust** tests. That is to say that they can still be used even if the data does not *quite* meet the requirement of parametric tests. This does not, however, mean that the requirements should be ignored and any test chosen whatever the data. Anyone who is very serious about the research you have done would notice if the requirements of normality of distribution and equality of variance have been completely ignored and use this to call the validity of your results into question.

Non-Parametric Tests are tests which make no assumptions about the populations from which the samples of data have been drawn. Their alternative title is '**distribution free**' statistics. This area of statistics grew rapidly in popularity when it was shown that the procedures are almost as good as parametric tests for small as well as large samples. (The larger a sample is, the closer it is to the population anyway, so the attraction of parametric procedures was that they gave good results with small samples. That is, until the development of good non-parametric tests for small samples.)

Requirements of all statistical tests
Because we have focused on parametric tests so far, we may have given the impression that non-parametric tests may be used on any old data. This is untrue, both types of test make some assumptions about the data you have obtained:
  • That the data has been obtained from a representative sample of the whole population, (or sometimes, the whole population itself).
  • That the study has been carried out with attention to detail, such as controlling unwanted variables etc.
  • That an appropriate and valid measure has been used to measure the variables in question.
Unless these requirements have been met, whichever type of test is performed on the data, it will produce results that have little meaning. (Garbage in - garbage out.)

Choosing a test
Before choosing a test you will need to know the design of your study, the type of data you will collect (or have collected) and something about the requirements of the tests. We have included

all of this in the flow charts on pages 12, 13 and 14:
1. Start on page 12 to **choose your test**.
2. Check that your **data is appropriate** on page 13.
3. Follow the chart on page 14 to **calculate your test**.

Note: You can still do a parametric test if your data does not meet the requirements of a parametric test. However, this is not very desirable given the advantages that parametric tests have over non-parametric tests. To return to the analogy used earlier, this would be like playing a brand new record on your old record player rather than the modern one. It would actually play it, but the results would not be as good and you might damage your record.

Using Statistical Tables

The last task to perform when carrying out a statistical procedure is looking up what's known as the critical value of the statistic you've just calculated. This is done using statistical tables and we've adapted some for your use at the end of this book. They can be a bit mystifying for the uninitiated, but like so many procedures in statistics, they are quite easy to use once you know how. Here's how...

The table comprises a list of values of the statistic in question which have already been worked out. They represent results which occur exactly on certain significance levels. The significance levels quoted are the ones most commonly used in social science research, i.e. $p \leq 0.05$ and $p \leq 0.01$ for both one and two-tailed hypotheses.

Note: Scrutiny of the tables will reveal the general rule that the probability level (not the critical value) is halved for a one-tailed hypothesis. This is because the test is looking for significance in only one half of the distribution with a one-tailed hypothesis. (See Sanders and Liptrot 1993.)

The F-Test at the end of the One-Way ANOVA, however, always assumes you have a two-tailed hypothesis, since it is looking for any pattern of differences in k samples (see page 89).

As you will discover, the calculations for the various statistics depend upon the number of scores collected, so at its most simple, you look up the value in the table that corresponds to the number of scores (usually called 'N') you have collected, at the significance level you have chosen (see page 23). The picture is slightly complicated by the fact that some tests ask you to work out what are called 'degrees of freedom' (df) rather than use N but this is usually very easy and is covered in the step-by-step guides to each test. Follow these steps:

1. Select the significance level, (see page 28.)
2. Note whether your hypothesis is one or two-tailed, get your N, df (or whatever the test requires) ready and turn to the appropriate table.
3. Find the column (or row) that corresponds to your significance level.
4. Find the row (or column) that corresponds to your N or df's.
5. You will find the appropriate critical value at the intersection of the row and column you've just chosen.

Inferential Statistics and Qualitative Research Methods

Research methods lie on a continuum from quantitative, empirical, measurement based 'objective' methods at one end to qualitative, process oriented, phenomenological, 'subjective' methods at the other. Whilst it is necessary for some books to polarise the differences to these extremes in order to explain them, we think that the real world of 'every day' research lies in the vast expanses of data collection and processing that lie between these extremes. Many studies are hybrids or employ both types of method alongside each other. There is nothing to stop you using inferential statistics at a later stage of data sorting and processing in a piece of qualitative research.

The present book is not an introduction to qualitative research methods, nor will it tell you how to use inferential statistics in conjunction with qualitative methods. If you wish to become familiar with qualitative research methods you should read, **An Incomplete Guide to Qualitative Research Methods for Counsellors** by Pete Sanders and Damian Liptrot (1994) published by PCCS (in press) or a similar publication. To get a good all round view of research methods and statistics for counsellors you will need a text that covers quantitative methods as well (see Sanders and Liptrot 1993).

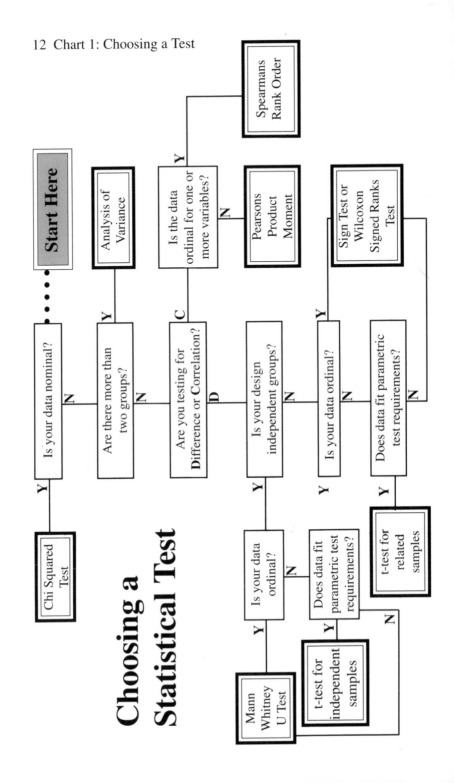

Choosing a
Statistical Test

Test Choice and Data Requirements

Type of test	Minimum data requirements	Nature of study			
		Two Independent Groups	More than two Independent Groups	Repeated Measures or Matched Pairs	Correlation
Non-Parametric Tests	Nominal (Frequency) Data	**Chi-squared test for difference**	**Chi-squared test for difference**		**Chi-squared test for association**
	Ordinal Data	**Mann Whitney U test**		**Sign Test or Wilcoxon Signed Ranks Test**	**Spearman's Rank Order Correlation**
Parametric Tests	Data must be: 1. Interval or Ratio. 2. Drawn from normally distributed population. 3. Equal variance in each sample.	**t-test for independent samples (Independent t-test)**	**One-way analysis of variance (ANOVA)**	**t-test for related samples (Related t-test)**	**Pearson's Product Moment Correlation**

Calculating a Statistical Test

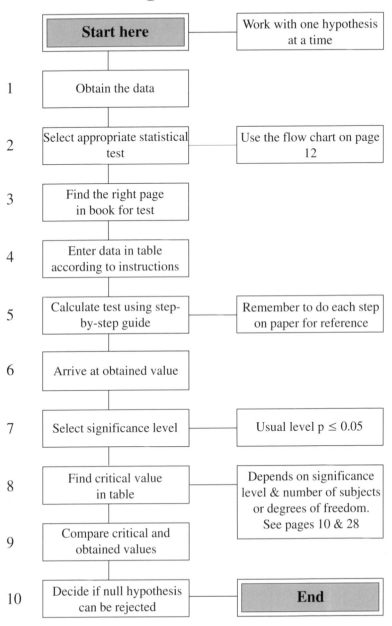

Start here — Work with one hypothesis at a time

1 Obtain the data

2 Select appropriate statistical test — Use the flow chart on page 12

3 Find the right page in book for test

4 Enter data in table according to instructions

5 Calculate test using step-by-step guide — Remember to do each step on paper for reference

6 Arrive at obtained value

7 Select significance level — Usual level $p \leq 0.05$

8 Find critical value in table — Depends on significance level & number of subjects or degrees of freedom. See pages 10 & 28

9 Compare critical and obtained values

10 Decide if null hypothesis can be rejected — End

Probability

"Probability is an obvious and simple subject. It is a baffling and complex subject...Such contradictions are the stuff of probability."
Kerlinger 1969

Probability and People - What does it have to do with me?
Probability is the word used to describe the *likelihood* that a particular event will occur. We say that "The *chances* are so-and-so" that something will happen, e.g:

> * Television weather forecasters have taken to making predictions like: "There is a 20% chance of rain in Manchester."
> * A friend of mine was told that they had an 80% chance of complete recovery after chemotherapy for cancer.

We arrange our thoughts, views about the world and behaviour in accordance with how we think such predictions will affect us. It is clear that we understand something about the nature of probability since we may hear two people talking about the football pools:

Person A: "I don't know why you do the pools - you'll never win!"
Person B: "Ah, no. *Everyone* has a chance of winning the jackpot."
A: "I know but it's about a million to one."
B: "Yes but it *could* happen."

We appreciate that there is something both absolute and variable about probability. It is subject to the laws and disciplines of mathematics. It obeys logic and allows us to predict events in the world, yet we flout the inherent rationality of probability when it suits us since most of us know a smoker who knows that smoking carries an increased risk of disease, disability and premature death, yet continues to smoke. Another person will refuse to fly even though they know that flying is the safest form of transport.

It's worth noting here that human beings enjoy a rather peculiar relationship with the concept of chance or 'likelihood'. Psychologists such as Hogarth (1980) and Kahneman et al. (1982) argue quite strongly that people do not think or act according to the laws of probability. They suggest that people make judgements according to certain heuristics or 'rules of thumb' regarding what we believe the laws of probability to be rather than what the laws of probability actually predict. It seems that we are prey to around seven or eight different kinds of bias when trying to predict things, including some familiar human traits such as *hindsight bias*, *overconfidence* and *frame effects* or the 'it-depends-how-you-look-at-it' factor. Here are a couple of examples:

1. Fischoff et al. in 1977 (see Hogarth) gave people a list of unfamiliar general knowledge statements and asked them how confident they were that the statements were true. Try it yourself:
   * Absinthe is a precious stone.
   * Playboy, not Time had the largest American circulation in 1970.
   * There are more deaths from pregnancy and childbirth than appendicitis.
   * The first air-raid was in 1849.
   * Potatoes are native to Ireland.

Respondents in the study were very confident that they knew the statements to be true. Did the respondents tell a lie? i.e. say they were confident when they weren't? Or are human beings just poorly calibrated measuring instruments of the truth of such statements, i.e. did they suffer from overconfidence? All the statements, by the way, are untrue.

2. Try the following two questions posed by Lovie (1983):
   a) Imagine you have decided to go to a concert where admission is £10.00 per ticket. As you wait in the ticket office queue you discover that you have lost a £10.00 note.

Would you still pay for a ticket for the concert, assuming you had enough money?
b) Imagine that you have bought a ticket to a concert for £10.00. As you wait to enter the concert hall you discover that you have lost the ticket. The ticket is unreserved and you have no proof of purchase. Would you pay £10.00 for another ticket, assuming you had enough money?

Financially there is no difference between the answers, but the frame of reference in each example is different. It is clear human beings respond to the contexts or frames of reference rather than the mathematics of the situation, since typically, 88% of subjects choose to buy the ticket in a) whereas only 46% would do so in b). This is known as a frame effect.

When conducting research we hope that we avoid these and other biases of being human by appealing direct to the laws of probability by using statistical procedures which will tell us how likely it is that our results are 'true'. Let's see how this happens.

By the way, it rained in Manchester and tragically, my friend died from cancer.

Probability and Numbers - What do the numbers mean?
Probability can be defined as: *'The degree to which an event is likely to occur.'* It's not enough, though, to simply say that there's a good, fair or poor chance that something will happen. We need to be able to quantify the likelihood of something happening. This is a process with which most of us are familiar, for example:
  * Bookmakers will give you the odds that a horse will win in terms of numbers, e.g. 10:1.
  * In common parlance we say that the chances are 50/50 that a coin will land heads.
  * We know that there's a one-in-four chance of picking a diamond from the top of a shuffled pack of cards (assuming that the jokers have been removed).

What do these numbers mean? The unfortunate fact is that mathematicians and statisticians do not use the same numbers to describe probability as we do in everyday language. However, the numbers they use are simple enough to understand and we need to understand them in order to understand the rationale behind inferential statistics. Look at the following statements and give each a value between 0 (impossible) and 100 (certain) depending upon how likely you think it is to occur:

1. Life will be discovered on Mars within 5 years.
2. The BAC membership will increase by over 500 individuals next year.
3. Choosing a red card from a fairly shuffled pack.
4. It will snow on Christmas day this year.
5. You will see a tiger this afternoon.
6. The sun will rise in the east tomorrow morning.

Two things can be learned from this activity:

Firstly, that everyone will come up with the same estimate for some statements, yet as you proceed, you will notice that for other statements, the estimate will depend upon a number of factors, including:

* who you are: a zoo keeper may feel fairly certain about number 5, and the membership secretary of BAC will feel on safe ground regarding number 2,

* where you are: people living in Reykjavik and Cairo will given different answers to number 4,

* and for number 1 for example, what you consider the term 'life' to mean.

Secondly, that putting numbers to the likelihood of events is really quite easy. Using a scale from 0 to 100 is very similar to the scale used by mathematicians and statisticians. The main difference is one of scale. Mathematicians and statisticians use a scale from 0 (impossible) to 1 (certain) to indicate the probability of a particular event occurring:

0	0.5	1
Impossible	Highly unlikely	Just as likely to happen as not	Highly likely	Certain

So just divide the answers you gave to the exercise above by 100 and you will be using the same numbering system as the statisticians.

Some of us are familiar with using *percentage probability*. This is where we might hear the weather forecaster say that there's a 20% chance of rain in Birmingham today. Also, in an abbreviated form of percentage probability we might say that there's a 50/50 chance of a coin landing 'heads'. This means that there's a 50% chance of a fairly tossed coin landing 'heads'. This percentage probability is a rather old fashioned way of talking about probability, and although we might use it in everyday language, in statistics we talk about probability in terms of a scale from 0 to 1.

Everyone should be familiar with a pack of cards, so here are some problems to get you used to working out simple probabilities:
    1. What is the probability of picking a red card from a fairly shuffled pack?
    2. What is the probability of picking a heart from a fairly shuffled pack?
    3. What is the probability of picking a picture card (jack, queen or king) from a fairly shuffled pack?
Some people will do numbers 1 and 2 in this exercise almost without thinking, but if you're not one of them, it may be a good idea to look at the mathematics behind these probabilities. (Number 3, by the way is a little more difficult.) *To work out the probabilities mathematically, you take the number of ways the desired event can occur and divide it by the total number of possible outcomes.*

$$p = \frac{\text{number of ways the desired event can occur}}{\text{total number of possible outcomes}}$$

1. $p = \dfrac{\text{number of ways of picking a red card}}{\text{number of cards in the pack}} = \dfrac{26}{52} = \dfrac{1}{2} = 0.5$

2. $p = \dfrac{\text{number of ways of picking a heart}}{\text{number of cards in the pack}} = \dfrac{13}{52} = \dfrac{1}{4} = 0.25$

3. $p = \dfrac{\text{number of ways of picking a picture card}}{\text{number of cards in the pack}} = \dfrac{12}{52} = 0.23$

(You may need a calculator for the last one.)

You may have spotted that there is one major problem with all of this. That is, that working out the probabilities of real life events occurring in day-to-day situations turns out to be much more complicated than working out the likelihood of drawing a particular card from a particular pack. In fact, the probability of occurrence of **some** real life events just can't be calculated at all using these mathematical principles, because the mathematics rely on a *finite* number of possibilities whereas real life presents us with near enough an *infinite* number of possibilities. You may have already guessed that as life's rich tapestry would have it, most of the events that counsellors might be interested in fall into this latter category.

However all is not lost or made impossibly complicated, since we can turn our previous calculations back-to-front to tell us how likely something is by including in the calculation the number of times the desired event has already occurred. We can work out the probability with which the event has occurred to date and we can assume that this level will hold true for the future. So we predict the future probability on the basis of past evidence. Sometimes this is called *empirical probability*.

$p = \dfrac{\text{number of times the event in question has occurred}}{\text{the total number of 'relevant' events which have occurred}}$

Everyday example: If we wanted to calculate the probability of snow falling in Birmingham on Christmas Day next year, we could calculate it as follows:

$p = \dfrac{\text{number of times it has snowed on Christmas Day in Birmingham}}{\text{number of Christmas Days since weather records began}}$

Counselling example: We could calculate the probability of a client experiencing the return of symptoms of anxiety after behavioural treatment as follows:

p = <u>number of clients reporting the return of symptoms after treatment</u>
total number of clients completing treatment

We would then be able to inform prospective clients of the **probable** success of the treatment.

This example demonstrates how probability and data collection can work together to predict an outcome. This is similar to generalising from a sample to a population - the basic task of research (see Sanders and Liptrot 1993):

When we generalise from a sample to a population, we say:
  "What holds true for the sample will hold true for the population."
When we use empirical probability to predict an outcome, we say:
  "What held true for the past will hold true for the future."

Now let's see how these ideas of the probability of an event occurring combine with statistical procedures to help us evaluate the usefulness of our data.

Probability and Statistics - Why use inferential statistics at all?

As we wrote in Section 1, inferential statistics help us make *inferences* from our data. We collect the data, then depending upon the exact nature of the events we measured, we work out how likely it is that the events we measured are due to chance, or some other effect. The 'some other effect' is usually the *independent variable* in an experiment, although it can be almost anything in everyday life. Inferential statistics are most commonly used alongside research methods; in particular, the quantitative method known as the *experimental method* (see Sanders and Liptrot 1993 p 102-114). It is possible, however, to use inferential statistical procedures on data collected in qualitative studies. The nature of the data, not the nature of the research method, determines what statistical procedures can be used.

Inferential statistics are based on probability and to make things easy for us, the mathematical procedures required are based on predetermined sets of calculations called statistical tests. These tests have been developed by statisticians over the years (often named after the person who first thought them up) and new ones are developed periodically. Statistical tests are, in principle, very simple. They work out the likelihood of a type of event by chance alone, then they compare your data to this chance figure. If it is unlikely that your data has occurred by chance then it is likely that something else is causing it. It is, however, our first guess that our results are due to chance factors (this is called the *null hypothesis* - see Sanders and Liptrot 1993 p96). Consider the following example:

A famous make of battery claims to last longer than its competitors. It demonstrates this by showing various battery operated toys working for longer when fitted with the advertised battery, whilst all the toys fitted with other batteries have long since stopped. We might, however ask the following questions:

1. Was the result shown in the advert a fluke? Does it happen every time? Or was it caused by chance fluctuations in battery performance.

2. For how much longer does the advertised battery run compared with its competitors? - 10 seconds, 10 minutes or longer?

3. How many batteries would we need to see tested before the results could be relied upon?

These questions are attempting the same task as statistical tests. The first one suggests that a repeatable effect is less likely (probability - remember?) to be the result of chance factors. The second is saying that a small effect is less likely (probability again) to indicate a real effect than a large effect. The third suggests that there is probably (!) an optimum number of tests required to convince us that the effect is real.

These (and other) questions can all be boiled down to the one question we all want answered:

"Is the effect 'real' or is it due to chance?"

In order to answer this question properly we would have to conduct an experiment (see Sanders and Liptrot 1993, p102-114) where the capabilities of the batteries were tested under controlled conditions. Still the dilemma remains.

Probability and Significance
Here are a couple of everyday examples where we can calculate the probability of the events being due to chance quite simply:

Example 1: Extra Sensory Perception?
You may have seen the 'serious' psychological study of ESP at the start of the film 'Ghostbusters' where the character played by Bill Murray looks at cards with symbols on and asks two subjects to read his mind and guess what symbols he is looking at. In the film the subjects are punished for wrong answers by being given increasingly painful electric shocks. Imagine we are doing a similar study without the shocks. We have five cards each with a different symbol printed on it. Let's say that we ask a subject to look at the freshly shuffled pack of five cards and guess which symbol is on the top card. Suppose we repeat the test ten times, shuffling the pack in between each test, not telling the subject how well they're doing as the test proceeds.

What pattern of results would you need in order to prove to your satisfaction that the subject was using **extra sensory perception** *(the experimental hypothesis) rather than* **chance guesswork** *(the null hypothesis)?*
* How many correct guesses would he or she have to make out of the 10 tests?

Our first task is to work out the results that we could expect from chance alone. We do this by working out the chance probability of success (see page 19) then applying it to the number of tests in our example:

In each test:

p = number of ways the desired event can occur
    total number of possible outcomes

p = number of ways of guessing the correct card = 1 = 0.2
              number of cards   5

So over 10 tests we would expect our 'subject' to get 10 x 0.2 = 2 correct guesses by chance.

This figure assumes that the 2 correct guesses do not come in a row. Now that we know that we could reasonably expect anyone to make 2 correct guesses by chance alone, how will we know when our results are **so** different from chance that we can reasonably say that the results might be due to Extra Sensory Perception?

Next we could work out how probable it is that our 'subject' makes 10 correct guesses. This is slightly more complicated since now we are assuming that the 10 correct guesses **do** come in a row! The subject has to get the first guess right (p = 0.2), and the second guess right (p = 0.2), and the third (another p = 0.2), and the fourth.....up to the tenth guess (a final p = 0.2) right. So we have to multiply 0.2 by 0.2 ten times to get the probability of making fifty successive correct guesses:

$p = (0.2)^{10}$ [This means 0.2 'to the power of 10' or 0.2 x 0.2 x 0.2 ten times over.]

If you work this out on a cheap calculator, it will give up after ten multiplications of 0.2 x 0.2 and just read 0. This means that the calculator can't handle such small numbers. (This is a big clue to the fact that the probability we're trying to work out is very small indeed.) On a good calculator the screen will read as follows:

p = 0.00000002048 [After 0.2 x 0.2 ten times.]

In 'everyday' numbers this means less than one chance in ten million.

> *To help put this figure in context; as I write, bookmakers are giving odds of one million to one that Screaming Lord Such will become Prime Minister, 10,000 to 1 that extra terrestrials will take over the earth next week and 250-1 that Elvis Presley will turn up alive. Such figures give general clues to commonly held views about the probabilities of events and further illustrate the peculiar and irrational relationship we humans have with probability.*

So, to get back to our problem, our decision lies somewhere between the probabilities of 0.2 and 0.00000002048. Perhaps by now you may be beginning to realise that however many calculations we make, the numbers will not help us in the end. We have to make the decision ourselves as to what level of probability we find acceptable. The more cautious or sceptical amongst us may veer towards the 0.00000002048 figure, whilst the more daring (or those that want to believe in ESP) will opt for something nearer 0.2. We must be careful to pitch our guess just right so that we don't make a mistake and either:

* Say that ESP is the cause when it really isn't, or
* Say that ESP isn't the cause when it really is!

These mistakes are known as Type I and Type II errors. They are the two types of error possible when selecting a significance level.

Type 1 error: This is when we claim that an effect is due to the independent variable (whatever we have manipulated in the experiment), when it is really due to chance. This sometimes happens when we choose a significance level that is too lax, i.e. too close to chance. It is not rigorous enough. Of course the closer the significance level is to chance, the easier it will before our results to achieve, so we have something of a dilemma as indicated above.

Type 2 error : This is when we set a significance level that is too rigorous, i.e. we think that the effect is due to chance when it is really due to the independent variable. This can happen if our sampling is poor, or our design slack. Alternatively, we might just have been too ambitious or overconfident in our selection of a significance level.

The consequences of these errors are quite serious since we would lose credibility if we said that effects existed when they did not and we would certainly miss out on the fame and fortune that would be the consequence of being the first to prove that ESP existed!

Whilst you're thinking about where you would draw the line and say "Yes for me the results now show that ESP is being used", think back to the last section on **Probability and People** and remember also that human beings aren't very good at working out probabilities because we tend to use illogical rules of thumb. The next example may be easier since it challenges you to take a more personal risk - money!

Example 2 : Pub 'con-artist'?
Imagine you are at the bar in a pub waiting for friends. You order a drink, but instead of asking for payment, the person serving you offers you a deal. She takes a coin from the till and suggests that you toss the coin. If it lands heads you pay double the price of the drink, if it lands tails you get the drink free.

You agree (possibly against your better judgement) and toss the coin. It lands heads. You pay double the cost of your lemon and lime.

Your friends are a little late, so you order another drink and are offered the same deal. You agree again, toss the coin and it lands heads a second time. The woman behind the bar commiserates with your bad luck and offers the same deal on your next drink, saying that you've got to win sometime.
You toss the coin, it lands heads. This is the third drink you've had to pay double for.

*How long would you put up with paying double for drinks before you rejected the idea that **the coin was fair**, i.e. that **chance was determining the outcome** (the null hypothesis) and you accepted the idea that **the barperson was cheating** in some way (the experimental hypothesis)?*
* How many times would the coin have to land 'heads' in a row?

Following the principle above, in this example we again work out the probability of a run of fair coin tosses then draw the line at the point at which we would not tolerate further loss and accuse the barperson of cheating. Some of us may find this a little easier!

The formula for each toss is:

$$p = \frac{\text{number of ways the desired event can occur}}{\text{total number of possible outcomes}}$$

$$p = \frac{\text{number of ways of getting heads}}{\text{total number of sides of the coin}}$$

$$p = \frac{1}{2} \quad = 0.5$$

and for each successive toss we multiply each previous probability by another 0.5.

So, for a consecutive run of heads:

1 toss	=	0.5 probability
2 tosses	=	0.25
3 tosses	=	0.125
4 tosses	=	0.0625
5 tosses	=	0.03125
6 tosses	=	0.015625
7 tosses	=	0.0078125
8 tosses	=	0.0039062
9 tosses	=	0.0019531
10 tosses	=	0.0009765 (around 10,000 - 1)

Where would you draw the line? Would you stop gambling at 4 tosses, 6 tosses...? The decision is, in many ways, a highly personal one. For each of us it reflects something of our personality (how risky we like to be and how much we enjoy gambling), our resourcing (some of us couldn't afford to gamble at a bar in this way), our views about the trustworthiness of bar staff, probability in the real world, and so on. *So how can research in the social sciences ever get past this personal (and therefore highly variable) decision?*

Choosing a Significance Level

You will have gathered by now that choosing a significance level seem caught between the devil and the deep blue sea. The way out of the dilemma is for all interested parties to agree to a loose convention.

In social science research it is convention to adopt a significance level of 0.05. This is expressed as $p \leq 0.05$ which means that the probability that the results are due to chance is **'less that or equal to'** 0.05. If you look back at the table of probabilities of a fair coin landing heads a number of times in succession on page 27, you will see that the 0.05 level is around four tosses. To get a sense of how possible this is, you may like to take a coin from your pocket or purse and toss it a few times.

> The 0.05 level is the same as a *5% probability* or the same as saying *one chance in twenty.*

You may not be happy with the convention of the 0.05 level, so significance levels other than the 0.05 level can be chosen if you want to be more certain of your results. For example, if you want to challenge a well established theory with your research, it is convention to choose a significance level of $p \leq 0.01$ or *1% probability* or *one chance in one hundred.* Also, would you be happy to let a drug on the market with only a 0.05 probability that it is *not* safe?

The tables in the back of this book enable you to find the critical values of statistics at both the 0.05 and 0.01 levels for both one and two tailed hypotheses.

The Chi-squared (χ^2)Test

When to use the Chi-squared Test

Chi-squared is a popular and well-known test. Whilst it has a number of applications, it is used only when the data obtained is nominal (sometimes referred to as *frequency data* or *categorical data*). So, the raw data for the test is how many subjects fall into each of the categories you have chosen.

In order to perform Chi-squared it must be possible to construct a *contingency table*, in which each possible behaviour is identified. For example, you may be interested in looking at whether people who have received counselling feel that their self esteem has increased and comparing them to people who have chosen not to receive counselling during the same period. Subjects either have or have not received counselling, and either judge themselves to have improved or not. Each of these possibilities (*contingencies*) can be entered into a contingency table. (See page 32)

It is possible to have a contingency table of just about any size. For example, you may be interested in looking at differences between social classes in the way they approach personal problems. This could yield the following 3 x 3 contingency table.

		CLASS		
		UPPER	MIDDLE	LOWER
APPROACH TO PROBLEMS	IGNORE THEM			
	GET VERY DRUNK			
	SEE A COUNSELLOR			

You could decide to use a 27 x 15 contingency table, but the calculation would be long-winded to say the least!

Limitations on the use of Chi-squared

The test deals in frequencies, so data must occur in that form - not percentages, fractions or ratios.

The Chi-squared test becomes unreliable in the following situations:
1. If the expected frequency in any cell is less than five in a 2 x 2 contingency table, the test cannot be used.
2. In larger contingency tables, if more than 20% of expected frequencies are less than five than the test should not be used.
3. Data must be independent, i.e. a score can occur in one cell only. Categories should be mutually exclusive and not overlap. In this regard, there may be a problem with the 'Approaches to Problems' in the 3 x 3 table illustrated, since a given subject might both get very drunk **and** see a counsellor. (Not at the same time, we hope!)

On page 34 we mention the use of Yates' correction when there is only one degree of freedom. Strictly speaking, Yates' correction need only be used if you have one degree of freedom **and** any expected frequency falls below ten.

What the test does and types of Chi-squared

In all applications of χ^2, what is being investigated is whether the number of people falling into each of the categories is significantly different from that which we would expect due to chance. In order to do this, the test compares the **observed** frequencies in each cell with the **expected** frequencies. If the differences are large, then these can be considered unlikely to be due to chance.

There are three different types of Chi-squared test to serve different purposes, and remember, in all cases, nominal data is required, and the data should fit into a contingency table.

A : Chi-squared test for difference

This would be appropriate when there is a variable that has been deliberately manipulated to create different experimental conditions, and therefore uses an *independent groups* design. Thus, in the counselling example given earlier, the data would be analysed using the chi squared test for difference, to discover whether or not there was a significant difference in the number of people from each group reporting improvement. If a significant result were obtained this would tell us that the difference in the numbers of people reporting an improvement was significant and that this was due to the independent variable (counselling or no counselling).

B : Chi-squared test for association
This application of chi squared is similar to the above, but would be used when the differences between the subjects were naturally occurring variables rather than the result of deliberate manipulation to create experimental conditions. For example introverts and extroverts would form two different groups, but this has not been manipulated by the experimenter. We may wish to look at whether introverts or extroverts were more likely to report marital difficulties or other problems to a counsellor. If the results of the chi squared analysis were significant, this would show an association (correlation) between personality and type of presenting problem that was unlikely to be caused by chance. However, we could not use the result to suggest that the personality type was the cause of the presenting problem.

C : Chi-squared test for goodness of fit
In the most frequent use of this application, subjects are presented with a number of choices, e.g. BAC members may be given a choice of four different topics for a seminar meeting. If there were no bias, each choice would occur an equal number of times. The test for goodness of fit will tell us whether or not the choices made by members differ significantly from what we would expect due to chance.

Note : *In all cases of the chi squared test, what is being investigated is whether or not the number of times each category of behaviour occurs (observed frequencies) differs from what would be expected as the result of chance factors (expected frequencies).*

Calculating the Chi-squared test

STEP 1: Produce a contingency table such as that shown below. The table should contain a square (*cell*) for each possible category of behaviour, i.e.

	RECEIVED COUNSELLING	RECEIVED NO COUNSELLING
INCREASED SELF ESTEEM		
NO INCREASE IN SELF ESTEEM		

STEP 2: Enter the observed frequencies of each behaviour into the appropriate cell of the contingency table. These are whatever figures you have obtained from your study for each cell of the contingency table.

STEP 3: Name each cell of the contingency table using a different letter for each. The top left hand cell should be called A and then the cell next to it B etc. (as shown below).

Example 1 (2 x 2 Contingency Table)

	RECEIVED COUNSELLING	NO COUNSELLING
INCREASED SELF ESTEEM	A	B
NO INCREASE IN SELF ESTEEM	C	D

Example 2 (3 x 3 Contingency Table)

		CLASS		
		UPPER	MIDDLE	LOWER
APPROACH TO PROBLEMS	IGNORE THEM	A	B	C
	AVOID DRUNK	D	E	F
	SEE A COUNSELLOR	G	H	I

STEP 4: Calculate the number of degrees of freedom (df) using the following formula :

df = (number of rows - 1) x (number of columns - 1)

Note : *If df = 1 then a slightly different calculation is required involving the use of a procedure known as Yates' Correction. This is dealt with within the guide to calculation.*

STEP 5: Add together the values of each of the cells to obtain the Grand Total:

For Example 1 above, this would be:
Grand Total = A + B + C + D

For Example 2 above, this would be:
Grand Total = A + B + C + D + E + F + G + H + I

STEP 6: For each row of the contingency table add together all the figures in the row to obtain a row total (as shown below).

STEP 7: For each column of the contingency table add together all the figures in the column to obtain a column total (as shown below).

Example 1 (2 x 2 Contingency Table)

	RECEIVED COUNSELLING	RECEIVED NO COUNSELLING	ROW TOTAL
INCREASED SELF ESTEEM	A	B	A+B
NO INCREASE IN SELF ESTEEM	C	D	C+D
COLUMN TOTAL	A+C	B+D	

Example 2 (3 x 3 Contingency Table)

		UPPER	CLASS MIDDLE	LOWER	ROW TOTAL
APPROACH TO PROBLEMS	IGNORE THEM	A	B	C	A+B+C
	GET VERY DRUNK	D	E	F	D+E+F
	SEE A COUNSELLOR	G	H	I	G+H+I
	COLUMN TOTAL	A+D+G	B+E+H	C+F+I	

STEP 8: Create a table such as the one below, leaving a line for each cell in the contingency table.

Note: *If χ^2 is being calculated with 1 df then the table headings are slightly different. These are shown inset in the table below:*

CELL TOT	ROW TOT	COLUMN TOTAL	GRAND TOTAL	OBSERVED FREQ	EXPECTED FREQ	OF-EF	(OF-EF)	$\dfrac{(OF\text{-}EF)^2}{EF}$
A B C D Etc						$(|OF\text{-}EF|\text{-}^1/_2)$	$(|OF\text{-}EF|\text{-}^1/_2)^2$	$\dfrac{(|OF\text{-}EF|^1/_2)^2}{EF}$

For 1df you need three columns with these headings (see text p35)

STEP 8 (continued): Stage by stage guide to the calculation.
For each cell in the contingency table
i) Enter the observed frequency (OF) for that cell in the
fifth column (observed frequency).
Remember, the observed frequencies are the figures
you first entered in the contingency table.
ii) Enter the row total for that cell in the second column
(ROW TOT)
iii) Enter the column total for that cell in the third
column. (COLUMN TOTAL)
iv) Enter the grand total for that cell in the fourth
column. (GRAND TOTAL)
Note : *The grand total will be the same for all cells.*
v) Calculate the expected frequency for that cell using
the following procedure:

$$\text{Expected frequency (EF)} = \frac{\text{Row total} \times \text{Column Total}}{\text{Grand Total}}$$

Note : *If any of your expected frequencies are less than
5, you should not proceed with the test. The way round
this is to either test more subjects or to see if any of the
categories in your contingency table can be combined.*
vi) Enter the expected frequency in the sixth column.
(Expected Frequency)
vii) Take away the expected frequency from the observed
frequency. Enter the number in the appropriate column in
the table, if the number has a minus sign in front of it,
ignore this and just write in the number.
In the table this is shown as OF - EF
viii) If there is more than one degree of freedom, skip
this stage:
> *For one degree of freedom only....*
> > Subtract 1/2 from the figure in the last column.
> > Enter this in the next column of the table.
> > [In the table this is shown as $(|OF\text{-}EF|\text{-}^1/_2)$]
Now simply continue with the calculation, though remember that
you will need different headings in your table [ones which
include the minus $^1/_2$ (see inset in table on page 34)].

ix) Square the figure obtained at the last stage. Enter the figure in the appropriate column of the table.
In the table this is shown as $(OF-EF)^2$
x) Divide the number obtained in the last stage by the expected frequency (EF). Enter the figure in the appropriate column of the table.
In the table this is shown as $\dfrac{(OF-EF)^2}{EF}$
xi) Repeat stages i to x for each cell.

STEP 9 : Add up all the figures in the final column. This gives the obtained value of χ^2

The formula for this is $\chi^2 = \displaystyle\sum \dfrac{(OF-EF)^2}{EF}$

STEP 10 : Compare the **obtained value** of χ^2 with the **critical value** of χ^2 shown in the table of critical values of χ^2 on page 102. The **critical value** of χ^2 will depend on the degrees of freedom (worked out in STEP 4) and whether your hypothesis is one or two tailed. *If the **obtained value** of χ^2 is greater than the **critical value** in the table on page 102, the null hypothesis can be rejected.*

A **significant result** indicates that the distribution of scores within the contingency table is different from that which would be expected due to chance. The interpretation of a significant result will depend on the application of the test.

A **test for difference** can conclude that there is a significant difference, and that this has been caused by the manipulation of the independent variable.

A **test for association** can conclude that there is a greater degree of association between the variables measured than would be expected due to chance alone, but not that one variable has had an **effect** upon the other.

Worked Example

This data is from a hypothetical study in which we wish to see if there is an association between receiving counselling and an increase in self-esteem. Seventy three students are chosen at random from the records of a University health service to see if they have received counselling. They were then asked if they had experienced an increase in self esteem. The same data is used here to demonstrate both tests for difference and tests of association, (the calculation is the same, only the hypotheses and conclusions are different). We could say, e.g. that we are looking for a *difference* in self esteem between those that have received counselling and those that have not.

STEP 1: Produce a contingency table (see below).

STEP 2: Enter the observed frequencies of each behaviour into the appropriate cell of the contingency table.

STEP 3: Name each cell of the contingency table using a different letter for each.

	RECEIVED COUNSELLING	RECEIVED NO COUNSELLING	ROW TOTAL
INCREASED SELF ESTEEM	(A) 25	(B) 10	(A+B) 35
NO INCREASE IN SELF ESTEEM	(C) 8	(D) 30	(C+D) 38
COLUMN TOTAL	(A+C) 33	(B+D) 40	

STEP 4: Calculate the number of degrees of freedom (df) as follows
df = (number of rows - 1) x (number of columns - 1)
Number of rows = 2
Number of columns = 2
df = (2 - 1) x (2 - 1)
df = 1 x 1
df = 1 (remember that Yates' Correction is needed for 1df)

STEP 5: Add together the values of each of the cells to obtain the Grand Total.
Grand Total = A + B + C + D
Grand Total = 25 + 10 + 8 + 30
Grand Total = 73

STEP 6: For each row of the contingency table add together all the figures in the row to obtain a row total (as shown in table above).

STEP 7: For each column of the contingency table add together all the figures in the column to obtain a column total (as shown above).

STEP 8: Draw a table, with a line for each cell in the contingency table.

Note : *As χ^2 is being calculated with 1df then the table headings include Yates' Correction: minus $^1/_2$ (see table on page 34).*

CELL	ROW TOT	COL TOT	GRAND TOT	OBS FREQ	EXP FREQ	OF-EF	$(|OF-EF|-^1/_2)$	$(|OF-EF|-^1/_2)^2$	$\dfrac{(|OF-EF|^1/_2)^2}{EF}$
A	35	33	73	25	15.82	9.18	8.68	75.34	4.762
B	35	40	73	10	19.18	9.18	8.68	75.34	3.928
C	38	33	73	8	17.18	9.18	8.68	75.34	4.385
D	38	40	73	30	20.82	9.18	8.68	75.34	2.511

STEP 8: (Stage by stage guide to the calculation.)

For each cell in the contingency table:

    i) Enter the observed frequency (OF) for that cell in the fifth column (marked OBS FREQ)
        Example: Cell A : Observed Frequency (OF) = 35
                Cell B : Observed Frequency (OF) = 10

    ii) Enter the row total for that cell in the second column (marked ROW TOT).
        Example: Cell A : Row Total = 35
                Cell B : Row Total = 35

    iii) Enter the column total for that cell in the third column (marked COL TOT)
        Example: Cell A : Column Total = 33
                Cell B : Column Total = 40

iv) Enter the Grand Total for that cell in the fourth column. (Marked GRAND TOT)
   Note : the Grand Total will be the same for all cells

   Example: Cell A : Grand Total = 73
              Cell B : Grand Total = 73

v) Calculate the Expected Frequency for that cell using the following procedure :

Expected Frequency (EF) = $\dfrac{\text{Row Total} \times \text{Column Total}}{\text{Grand Total}}$

Example :   Cell A: EF = $\dfrac{35 \times 33}{73}$

            EF = 15.82 (to 2 decimal places)

            Cell B: EF = $\dfrac{35 \times 40}{73}$

            EF = 19.18 (to 2 decimal places)

vi) Enter the expected frequency in the sixth column (marked EXP FREQ).

vii) Take away the Expected Frequency from the observed frequency. Enter the number in the appropriate column of the table, if the number has a minus sign in front of it, ignore this, and just write in the number.
       Example : Cell A :   EF - OF = 25 - 15.82
                              EF - OF = 9.18

                 Cell B :   EF - OF = 10 - 19.18
                              EF - OF = -9.18

Note: Remember to ignore the minus sign before entering the figure in the table.
Also: In this example, all the differences (EF - OF) have worked out the same, this does not always happen.

viii) As there is 1 degree of freedom, we have used Yates' Correction and so this stage has been included, otherwise we would have skipped to the next stage of the calculation. Subtract $^1/_2$ from the figure in the last column. Enter the result in the next column of the table.

Example : Cell A : $(|EF - OF| - ^1/_2) = 9.18 - 0.5$

$\qquad (|EF - OF|) - ^1/_2) = 8.68$

Continue to repeat the calculation for the remaining cells, though remember that the $- ^1/_2$ will keep appearing in the table headings.

ix) Square the figure obtained in the last stage viii. Enter the figure in the appropriate column of the table.

Example : Cell A : $(|EF - OF| - ^1/_2)^2 = 8.68 \times 8.68$

$\qquad = 75.34$ (to 2 decimal places)

x) Divide the number obtained in the last stage by the expected frequency (EF). Enter the figure in the appropriate column of the table.

Example : $\dfrac{(|EF - OF| - ^1/_2)^2}{EF} = \dfrac{75.34}{15.82}$

$\qquad = 4.762$ (to 3 decimal places)

xi) Repeat stages i to x for each cell.

STEP 9 : Add up all the figures in the final column. This gives the **obtained value** of χ^2

The formula for this is $\chi^2 = \sum \dfrac{(|OF - EF| - ^1/_2)^2}{EF}$

Cell A $= 4.762$
Cell B $= 3.928$
Cell C $= 4.385$
Cell D $= 2.511$

Total $= 15.586 = \chi^2$

STEP 10: Compare the **obtained value** of χ^2 with the **critical value** of χ^2 shown in the table of critical values of χ^2 on page 102. The **critical value** of χ^2 will depend on the degrees of freedom (worked out in *STEP 4*). The hypothesis is two-tailed.
*Note: If the **obtained value** of χ^2 is greater than the **critical value** given in the table on page 102, the null hypothesis can be rejected.*

From the table of critical values of Chi-squared on page 102:
For χ^2 with 1 degree of freedom and a two-tailed hypothesis: the critical value for significance level $p \leq 0.05$ (5%) is 3.841. (See page 10, 'Using Statistical Tables'.)
Since the **obtained value** of χ^2 (15.586) is larger than the **critical value**, we can reject the null hypothesis.

We can thus claim:
either that there is a significant association between receiving counselling and reports of increase in self esteem,
or that there is a significant difference between the number of people who report increased self esteem depending upon whether they have or have not undergone counselling.

Whichever conclusion we could draw would depend on whether the two groups have been deliberately created, or have occurred naturally. In the case of deliberately created groups, a variable has been deliberately manipulated to create two experimental conditions (experimental method), therefore we would be looking for a difference rather than an association (typical of a correlation method).

Chi Squared for goodness of fit

In all the previous examples of Chi squared it has been used where there are at least two groups of subjects. However, it may be the case that you have one group of subjects who are offered a number of different options.
For example: A sample of 100 BAC members are asked where they would like the next BAC Conference to be held. They are then offered four different options, of which they may choose only one. Draw a table as shown overleaf:

Cell	Location	Number
A	London	15
B	Paris	10
C	Manchester	25
D	Wigan	50

The numbers of subjects making each choice (e.g. London = 15) become our observed frequencies.

We would then use the Chi squared test for goodness of fit to discover whether the number of people making each choice is different from what we would expect due to chance.
Note: Calculating Chi squared for goodness of fit is much simpler than the other versions of the test so the calculation guide and worked example will be covered together.

STEP 1: Create a table with the following headings, leaving a line for each choice offered to subjects.

Cell	OF	EF	OF - EF	$\dfrac{OF - EF}{EF}$	$\left(\dfrac{OF - EF}{EF}\right)^2$
A	15	25	10	0.4	0.16
B	10	25	15	0.6	0.36
C	25	25	0	0	0
D	50	25	25	1	1

Total = 1.52

STEP 2: For each cell enter the observed frequency (number of people making that choice) into the second column.

STEP 3: Calculate the expected frequencies. This is done simply by dividing the number of subjects by the number of choices. The expected frequencies for each cell will be identical, e.g.

$$EF = \frac{\text{Number of subjects}}{\text{Number of choices}} = \frac{100}{4} = 25$$

Enter the expected frequencies in the third column.

STEP 4: For each cell: Calculate OF - EF (subtract the figure in the third column from the figure in the second column). Enter these values in the appropriate column.
Note: *You can ignore any minus signs.*

STEP 5: For each cell: Divide the figure in the fourth column (OF - EF) by the figure in the third column (EF). Enter these figures in the appropriate column.

STEP 6: For each cell: Square the figure in the fifth column and enter the result in the final column.

STEP 7: Add up all the scores in the final column. This gives the obtained value of chi squared.
In this example this is $\chi^2 = 1.52$

STEP 8 : Calculate the degrees of freedom (df).
df = number of choices - 1 = 4 - 1 (in our example)
df = 3

STEP 9 : Using the table on page 102 look up the **critical value**. This will depend on the degrees of freedom, the level of significance chosen (usually $p \leq 0.05$) and whether the hypothesis is one or two-tailed.

If the **obtained value** is greater than (or equal to) the **critical value**, reject the null hypothesis i.e. the (distribution) number of people making each of the choices is significantly different than what would be expected due to chance.
In the example:
for df = 3, $p \leq 0.05$ with a two-tailed hypothesis,
critical value = 7.82

As the **obtained value** of 1.52 is less than the **critical value** we cannot reject the null hypothesis, and must conclude that the number of people choosing each of the destinations is not significantly different from what would be expected due to chance.

The Mann-Whitney U Test

When to use the Mann-Whitney Test.

The Mann Whitney Test is a non-parametric test for use on data obtained from experiments using an independent groups design. The data should at least be ordinal (subjects can score more or less than each other on some scale). The test can be used instead of a t-test for independent samples even when the requirements for the parametric test are met, but the only real reason for doing this would be to save time (have you seen the formula for the t-test?).

What the Mann-Whitney Test does

Quite simply, the scores in each condition are converted to ranks. As all subjects were taken from the same sample of the population and all then randomly assigned to one of the experimental conditions, if the independent variable has had an effect, we would expect that subjects in one condition would tend to score higher than subjects in the other condition. The test therefore looks at whether one of the conditions contains the majority of the higher ranking scores than the other condition. If each condition contains a mixture of high and low ranking scores, then the independent variable has had little effect and any difference between the scores is non-significant.

Note: In conducting the calculation two values of U are obtained (U_1 and U_2). This is because the calculation relies on the sum of the ranks of the smaller group (R_1) to calculate U_1. If the smaller of the two groups contains the larger scores and therefore the larger ranks, this will produce a small value for U_1.

If however, the smaller group contains the smaller scores and lower ranks, this will produce a high value of U_1 which is not likely to be significant. Calculating a second value (U_2) takes into account the fact that perhaps the ranks of the scores in the larger group should have been used in the calculation.

If each group contains a mixture of higher and lower scores and therefore high and low ranks, there will be little difference between the values of U_1 and U_2 and the result is unlikely to be significant.

Calculating the Mann-Whitney U Test

STEP 1: Construct a table containing four columns. (See p 47)

STEP 2: Enter the data from Condition A into the first column of the table, and the data from the other condition into the third column.

STEP 3: Rank all the scores from the lowest (Rank 1) to the highest (Rank n). Rank all the scores together as if they all come from one group; so the lowest score could be in one condition, the next score in the other condition and so on.

STEP 4: Count the number of scores in the smallest group, call this figure N_1. Count the number of scores in the largest group, call this figure N_2.
Note. *If there are the same number of scores in both groups choose either of the groups to be N_1.*

STEP 5: Add up all the **ranks** belonging to the smallest group (or whichever you have chosen). Call this figure R_1.

You should now have calculated the following:
N_1 = number of scores in the smallest group
N_2 = number of scores in the largest group
R_1 = sum of the ranks in the smallest group

STEP 6: Substitute the above values in the equation and calculate the obtained value U_1

$$U_1 = N_1 N_2 + \frac{N_1 (N_1+1)}{2} - R_1$$

i) Multiply the number of scores in the smaller group by the number of the scores in the larger group. In the equation this is shown as $N_1 N_2$

ii) Add 1 to the number of scores in the smaller group.
In the equation this is shown as (N_1+1)

iii) Multiply the number you have just obtained in stage ii by the number of scores in the smaller group.
In the equation this is shown as $N(N_1+1)$

iv) Divide the number you have just obtained by 2.
In the equation this is shown as $\dfrac{N(N_1+1)}{2}$

v) Add the number you have just obtained in stage vi to the number obtained in stage i.
In the equation this is shown as

$$\dfrac{N_1N_2+N_1(N_1+1)}{2}$$

vi) Subtract R_1 (sum of the ranks in the smaller group) from the figure obtained in stage v.
The equation is now complete:

$$U_1 = N_1\,N_2 + \dfrac{N_1\,(N_1+1)}{2} - R_1$$

You now have your value of U_1

STEP 7: Substitute the values of N_1 N_2 and U_1 in the following formula and calculate the second obtained value of U_2.
$$U_2 = N_1 N_2 - U_1$$

i) Multiply the number of scores in the smaller group by the number of scores in the larger group.
In the equation this is shown as $N_1 N_2$

ii) Subtract U_1 from the figure obtained in stage i
In the equation this is shown as $N_1 N_2 - U_1$
You now have your value of U_2

STEP 8: Select whichever is the smaller of U_1 and U_2
This is your final **obtained value**.

STEP 9: Find the **critical value** of U in the table on page 103, this will depend on the values of N_1 and N_2. (See p 10.)

STEP 10: Compare the **obtained value** (U_1 or U_2) with the **critical value**. If the obtained value is less than the critical value, reject the null hypothesis.

Worked Example

Practising counsellors were randomly divided into two groups. Group 1 (Condition A) were shown a video of Carl Rogers immediately prior to a session with a client, whilst Group 2 (Condition B) were shown a video of Albert Ellis. For each counsellor the number of empathic responses to the client during the following session were counted. The experimental hypothesis proposes that there will be a significant difference in the number of empathic responses made by the counsellor depending on which of the videos they had seen previously.

SCORES IN COND A	RANKS OF SCORES IN COND A	SCORES IN COND B	RANKS OF SCORES IN COND B
27	21	12	6.5
19	14.5	5	1
21	17	15	8.5
17	12	9	4
35	23	25	19.5
25	19.5	10	5
32	22	17	12
20	16	7	3
22	18	12	6.5
17	12	6	2
15	8.5	16	10
		19	14.5

STEPS 1 to 3 have been completed in the table above.

STEP 4: $N_1 = 11$ $N_2 = 12$
Count all the scores in the smallest group; call the figure N_1
Count all the scores in the largest group; call this figure N_2

STEP 5: $R_1 = 183.5$
Add up all the ranks belonging to the smallest group; call this figure R_1

In the example Condition A is the smallest group.

The following examples have been calculated:

$N_1 = 11$ = number of scores in the smallest group
$N_2 = 12$ = number of scores in the largest group
$R_1 = 183.5$ = sum of the ranks in the smallest group

STEP 6: Substitute the above values in the equation and calculate the obtained value U_1
$$U_1 = N_1 N_2 + \frac{N_1 (N_1+1)}{2} - R_1$$

i) 11 x 12 = 132
(Multiply the number of scores in the smaller group by the number of scores in the larger group.)

ii) 11 + 1 = 12
(Add 1 to the number of scores in the smaller group.)

iii) 11 x 12 = 132
(Multiply the number just obtained in stage ii by the number of scores in the smaller group.)

vi) 132 /2 = 66
(Divide the number you have just obtained in stage iii by 2.)

v) $132 + 66 = 198$
Add the number you have just obtained to the number
you obtained in stage iii.

vi) $198 - 183.5 = 14.5$
Subtract R_1 (sum of the ranks in the smaller group)
from the figure obtained in stage v.
This is the value of U_1

STEP 7: Substitute the values of N_1, N_2 and U_1 in the following
formula and calculate the second obtained value U_2

$$U_2 = N_1 N_2 - U_1$$

i) $11 \times 12 = 132$
(Multiply the number of scores in the smaller group
by the number of scores in the larger group.)

ii) $132 - 14.5 = 117.5$
Subtract U_1 from the figure obtained in stage i.
You now have your value of U_2

STEP 8: $U_1 = 14.5$ $\qquad$ $U_2 = 117.5$
U_1 is the smaller value. This is your final **obtained value**.

STEP 9 : From the table of critical values of U on page 103, when
$N_1 = 11$ and $N_2 = 12$, the **critical value** of U is 33

STEP 10 : As the **obtained value** U_1 (14.5) is less than the **critical
value** of U (33), the null hypothesis is rejected and the difference
between the scores in the two conditions is significant.

*Note : All critical values for the Mann Whitney test given in the
table are for two-tailed hypotheses. If your hypothesis is one-tailed
the significance level should be halved , i.e. from $p \leq$ 0.01 to
$p \leq$ 0.05, but the critical value remains unchanged.*

t-Test for Independent Samples (Independent t-Test)

When to use the Independent t-Test

The t-test is the most powerful of the tests covered in this section. If there is a significant difference, it is the test most likely to detect it. The test should therefore be the first choice whenever the data had been obtained in an experiment using an independent groups design. However, because it is a parametric test it makes greater requirements of the data on which it will operate satisfactorily. Firstly, the data should be interval or ratio, secondly the data should be drawn from a normal distribution, and lastly, there should be equal variance (spread) of the two sets of scores. Because the t-test is robust, it is not necessary to meet these requirements completely, but the data should not be too far removed from the requirements.

It is possible to calculate a Mann Whitney test using the same data, but as this is a less powerful test, you would only choose to do this to save time and effort. This is not a very good reason if you wish your research to be taken seriously.

What the Independent t-Test Does

The t-test gains greater power to detect significant differences (where they exist) by the fact that it makes full use of the data rather than converting it into ranks, which is what the non-parametric alternative Mann Whitney test does.

Basically, the test looks at the difference between the mean scores of the two groups of subjects. However, while the difference between the two means may appear larger enough to be regarded as significant, it is also important to look at the spread of the scores in the two conditions. If there is a large spread of scores in the two conditions, there would be considerable overlap between the results in the two conditions. The t-test takes the variance of the scores into account when deciding whether the difference between the two means is large enough to be regarded as significant.

Note: While you may have found the above jolly interesting, please don't try using it as a conversation starter in the pub or at dinner parties, the likelihood is that you will not be invited back.

Calculating the Independent t-Test

Before starting to calculate the test, draw a simple table with the headings as shown below.

Scores in Condition A	Squared Scores in Condition A	Scores in Condition B	Squared Scores in Condition B

STEP 1: Enter the scores for Condition A into the first column of the table.

STEP 2: Add up all the scores in Condition A. This gives ΣA.

STEP 3: Find the mean of the scores in Condition A by dividing the total of the scores by nA (number of subjects in condition A). This figure is $\overline{A}$

STEP 4: Square each of the scores in Condition A. Enter these into the second column of the table.

STEP 5: Add up all the squares of the scores from Condition A. This figure is ΣA^2

STEP 6: Enter the scores for Condition B into the third column of the table.

STEP 7: Add up all the scores in Condition B.
This figure is ΣB

STEP 8: Find the mean of the scores in Condition B by dividing the total of the scores by nB (number of subjects in Condition B)
This figure is $\overline{B}$

STEP 9: Square each of the scores from Condition B. Enter these into the fourth column of the table.

STEP 10: Add up all the squares of the scores from Condition B.
This figure is ΣB^2

You should now have calculated the following values:

ΣA $\quad$ = Sum of scores in Condition A
nA $\quad$ = Number of subjects in Condition A
$\overline{A}$ $\quad$ = Mean of scores in Condition A
ΣA^2 = Sum of the squared scores from Condition A

ΣB $\quad$ = Sum of scores in Condition B
nB $\quad$ = Number of subjects in Condition B
$\overline{B}$ $\quad$ = Mean of scores in Condition B
ΣB^2 = Sum of the squared scores from Condition B

STEP 11: Calculate the obtained value of *t* by substituting the above values in the following formula. Label each stage as you go through.

$$t = \frac{\overline{A} - \overline{B}}{\sqrt{\left(\frac{[\Sigma A^2 - (\Sigma A)^2/nA] + [\Sigma B^2 - (\Sigma B)^2/nB]}{(nA - 1) + (nB - 1)}\right)\left(\frac{1}{nA} + \frac{1}{nB}\right)}}$$

It would be entirely understandable if this looks a little off-putting, (to say the least) but we've broken it down into simple stages and if followed through stage by stage is not very difficult at all. It is however, as we have already pointed out, time consuming.

i) Square ΣA (the sum of all the scores in Condition A). This gives $(\Sigma A)^2$

ii) Calculate $(\Sigma A)^2/nA$ by dividing the figure you obtained in step i by nA (number of subjects in Condition A).

iii) Subtract the figure you have just calculated from ΣA^2 (sum of the squared scores in Condition A) to give $[\Sigma A^2 - (\Sigma A)^2/nA]$.

iv) Square ΣB (the sum of all the scores in Condition B). This gives $(\Sigma B)^2$.

v) Calculate $(\Sigma B)^2/nB$ by dividing the figure you obtained in step iv by nB (number of subjects in Condition B).

vi) Subtract the figure you have just calculated from ΣB^2 (sum of the squared scores in Condition B) to give $[\Sigma B^2 - (\Sigma B)^2/nB]$.

vii) Add together the figures obtained in stages iii and vi. This gives $[\Sigma A^2 - (\Sigma A)^2/nA] + [\Sigma B^2 - (\Sigma B)^2/nB]$.

viii) Subtract 1 from nA (number of subjects in Condition A) to get (nA - 1).

ix) Subtract 1 from nB (number of subjects in Condition B) to get (nB - 1).

x) Add together the figures obtained in stages viii and xi. This gives (nA - 1) + (nB - 1).

xi) Divide the figure obtained in stage vii by the figure obtained in stage x.

You now have worked out

$$\left(\frac{[\Sigma A^2 - (\Sigma A)^2/nA] + [\Sigma B^2 - (\Sigma B)^2/nB]}{(nA - 1) + (nB - 1)} \right)$$

xii) Divide 1 by nA (number of subjects in Condition A) to get $\dfrac{1}{nA}$

xiii) Divide 1 by nB (number of subjects in Condition B) to get $\dfrac{1}{nB}$

xiv) Add together the figures you have just obtained in stages xii and xiii to give $\left(\dfrac{1}{nA} + \dfrac{1}{nB} \right)$

xv) Multiply the figure obtained in stage xi by the figure obtained in stage xiv to give

$$\left(\frac{[\Sigma A^2 - (\Sigma A)^2/nA] + [\Sigma B^2 - (\Sigma B)^2/nB]}{(nA - 1) + (nB - 1)} \right)\left(\frac{1}{nA} + \frac{1}{nB} \right)$$

xvi) Find the square root of the figure you have just obtained.

xvii) Subtract $\overline{B}$ (mean of scores in Condition B) from $\overline{A}$ (mean of scores in Condition A). You can find this on the top line of the original formula as $\overline{A} - \overline{B}$

xviii) Divide the figure you have just obtained in stage xvii by the figure obtained in stage xvi. This is the **obtained value** of t calculated from the formula shown in *STEP 11* on page 52.

STEP 12: Calculate the degrees of freedom (df).

Add together nA (number of subjects in Condition A) and nB (number of subjects in Condition B) the subtract 2 from the number you have just obtained.

This can be shown as:

degrees of freedom (df) = (nA + nB) - 2

STEP 13 : Select the significance level. (The usual significance level is p ≤ 0.05).

STEP 14: Using the table of critical values of *t* on page 104, find the **critical value**. This will depend on number of degrees of freedom and the level of significance.

STEP 15: Compare the **obtained value** you calculated from the test with the **critical value** given in the table. If the **obtained value** is larger than, or equal to the **critical value**, you can reject the null hypothesis and say that the difference between the two sets of scores is significant.

Worked Example

In this example we are studying two groups of subjects. Condition A is made up of couples who are waiting for counselling and Condition B is made up of couples who have undergone counselling. The couples are asked to measure the amount of time they spend ignoring each other during the week.

The independent variable is the status of the couple (waiting for counselling or having undergone counselling). The dependent variable is length of time spent ignoring each other (measured in hours). The data is therefore ratio data.

Scores in Condition A	Squared Scores in Condition A	Scores in Condition B	Squared Scores in Condition B
17	289	12	144
19	361	15	225
21	441	15	225
17	289	19	361
17	289	9	81
25	625	25	625
15	225	10	100
32	1024	17	289
20	400	17	289
22	484	12	144
17	289	6	36
15	225	16	256

STEP 1: Performed in the table above. Scores in Condition A are entered into column 1.

STEP 2: Sum of scores in Condition A. $\Sigma A = 237$

STEP 3: Find the mean of scores in Condition A.
$$\overline{A} = \frac{\Sigma A}{nA} = \frac{237}{12} = 19.75$$

STEP 4: Performed in the table above. Squared Condition A scores are entered into column 2.

STEP 5: Sum of squared Condition A scores $\Sigma A^2 = 4941$

STEP 6: Performed in the table above. Scores in Condition B are entered into column 3.

STEP 7: Sum of scores in Condition B. $\Sigma B = 17$

STEP 8: Find the mean of scores in Condition B

$$\overline{B} = \frac{\Sigma B}{nB} = \frac{173}{12} = 14.42$$

STEP 9: Performed in the table above. Squared Condition B scores are entered into column 4.

STEP 10: Sum of squared Condition B scores $\Sigma B^2 = 2775$.

You should now have calculated the following values:

$\Sigma A = 237$	Sum of scores in Condition A
$nB = 12$	Number of subjects in Condition A
$\overline{A} = 19.75$	Mean of scores in Condition A
$\Sigma A^2 = 4941$	Sum of the squared scores from Condition A
$\Sigma B = 173$	Sum of scores in Condition B
$nB = 12$	Number of subjects in Condition B
$\overline{B} = 14.42$	Mean of scores in Condition B
$\Sigma B^2 = 2775$	Sum of the squared scores from Condition B

STEP 11 : Calculate the obtained value of *t* by substituting the above values in the following formula:

$$t = \frac{\overline{A} - \overline{B}}{\sqrt{\left(\frac{[\Sigma A^2 - (\Sigma A)^2/nA] + [\Sigma B^2 - (\Sigma B)^2/nB]}{(nA - 1) + (nB - 1)}\right)\left(\frac{1}{nA} + \frac{1}{nB}\right)}}$$

i) Square ΣA (the sum of all the scores in condition A). This gives $(\Sigma A)^2 = 56169$

ii) Calculate $(\Sigma A)^2/nA$ by dividing the figure you obtained in step i by nA (number of subjects in Condition A).

$(\Sigma A)^2/nA = \frac{56169}{12} = 4680.75$

iii) Subtract the figure you have just calculated from ΣA^2 (sum of the squared scores in Condition A) to give
$[\Sigma A^2 - (\Sigma A)^2/nA] = 4941 - 4680.75 = 260.24$

iv) Square ΣB (sum of all the scores in Condition B). This gives $(\Sigma B)^2 = 29929$

v) Calculate $(\Sigma B)^2/nB$ by dividing the figure you obtained in step vi by nB (number of subjects in Condition B) to give
$(\Sigma B)^2/nB = \dfrac{29929}{12} = 2494.1$

vi) Subtract the figure you have just calculated from ΣB^2 (sum of the squared scores in Condition B) to give
$[\Sigma B^2 - (\Sigma B)^2/nB] = 2775 - 2494.1 = 280.9$

vii) Add the figures obtained in stages iii and vi. This gives $[\Sigma A^2 - (\Sigma A)^2/nA] + [\Sigma B^2 - (\Sigma B)^2/nB]$
$= 260.24 + 280.9 = 541.14$

viii) Subtract 1 from nA (number of subjects in condition A) to get $(nA - 1) = 12 - 1 = 11$

ix) Subtract 1 from nB (number of subjects in condition B) to get $(nB - 1) = 12 - 1 = 11$

x) Add the figures obtained in stages viii and ix. This gives $(nA - 1) + (nB - 1) = 11 + 11 = 22$

xi) Divide the figure obtained in stage vii by the figure obtained in stage x:
$$\dfrac{[\Sigma A^2 - (\Sigma A)^2/nA] + [\Sigma B^2 - (\Sigma B)^2/nB]}{(nA - 1) + (nB - 1)} = \dfrac{541.14}{22} = 24.6$$

xii) Divide 1 by nA (number of subjects in
Condition A) to get $\dfrac{1}{nA} = \dfrac{1}{12} = 0.0833$

xiii) Divide 1 by nB (number of subjects in
Condition B) to get $\dfrac{1}{nB} = \dfrac{1}{12} = 0.0833$

xiv) Add together the figures you have just obtained
in stages xii and xiii to give

$$\left(\frac{1}{nA} + \frac{1}{nB} \right) = 0.0833 + 0.0833 = 0.1666$$

xv) Multiply the figure obtained in stage xi by the
figure obtained in stage xiv to give

$$\left(\frac{[\Sigma A^2 - (\Sigma A)^2/nA] + [\Sigma B^2 - (\Sigma B)^2/nB]}{(nA - 1) + (nB - 1)} \right) \left(\frac{1}{nA} + \frac{1}{nB} \right)$$

$= 24.6 \times 0.1666 = 4.098$

xvi) Find the square root of the figure you have just
obtained

$\sqrt{4.098} = 2.024$

xvii) Subtract $\overline{B}$ (mean of scores in Condition B)
from $\overline{A}$ (mean of scores in Condition A).
$\overline{A} - \overline{B} = 19.75 - 14.42 = 5.33$

xviii) Divide the figure you have just obtained in stage
xvii by the figure obtained in stage xvi. This is the
obtained value of t calculated from the formula shown
in *STEP 11* on page 57.

Obtained value of $t = \dfrac{5.33}{2.024} = 2.633$

STEP 12: Calculate the degrees of freedom (df).
Add together nA (number of subjects in Condition A) and nB (number of subjects in Condition B) the subtract 2 from the number you have just obtained.

$$df = (nA + nB) - 2 = (12 + 12) - 2 = 24 - 2 = 22$$

$$df = 22$$

STEP 13: Significance level $= 5\%$ ($p \leq 0.05$) for a two-tailed test.

STEP 14: From the table of critical values of t on page 104, the **critical value** of t with 22 df $= 2.074$

STEP 15: As the **obtained value** of t ($t = 2.633$) is larger than the **critical value** of t ($t = 2.074$), we can reject the null hypothesis; the difference between the two sets of scores is significant.

Note: As the mean of the scores in Condition A (19.75) is higher than the mean of the scores in Condition B (14.42), it can also be concluded that couples who have not undergone counselling spend significantly more time ignoring each other than couples who have undergone counselling.

STEP 6 : Using the table on page 105 look up the **critical value**. This will depend on N (number of subjects) and the chosen significance level see page 28.

STEP 7 : Compare the **obtained value** of x with the **critical value** from the table. If **obtained value** is less than or equal to the **critical value**, reject the null hypothesis.

Worked Example

In this experiment, subjects have been observed in conversation with a counsellor (Condition A), and with a person who is not a counsellor (Condition B). During the first five minutes of the conversation, the times taken to respond to a question are measured and an average taken. We are interested in finding out if there is a significant difference between the time taken to respond to a counsellor and the time taken to respond to a person who is not a counsellor. At this stage we predict that there will be a difference, but have not predicted the direction of the difference. This is a two-tailed hypothesis (see Sanders and Liptrot 1993, p98-100). The null hypothesis is that there will be no significant difference in the time taken to respond to counsellors and non-counsellors.

SUBJECT	SCORES IN CONDITION A	SCORES IN CONDITION B	DIRECTION OF DIFFERENCES
1	17	12	+
2	19	15	+
3	21	15	+
4	17	19	-
5	17	9	+
6	25	25	0omitted
7	15	10	+
8	32	17	+
9	20	17	+
10	22	12	+
11	17	6	+
12	15	16	-

STEPS 1 & 2 have been conducted on the table.

STEP 3 : The minus sign (-) is the sign occurring least frequently. There are 2 differences with the - sign. Therefore x = 2. *This is the obtained value.*

STEP 4 : N = 11. There are 12 sets of scores, but one set has produced no difference therefore it is excluded from the calculation, leaving 11.

STEP 5 : The usual significance level is 5% (p $\leq$ 0.05).

STEP 6 : From the table on page XX where N = 11 and the significance level is 5% (p $\leq$ 0.05), for a two-tailed hypothesis:

The **critical value** given in the table is 1

STEP 7 : As the **obtained value** (x = 2) is greater than the **critical value** given in the table (x=1), the null hypothesis cannot be rejected, thus indicating that the difference between the scores in the 2 conditions of the experiment is not significant.

Since we are accepting the null hypothesis, we can conclude that there is no difference between the times taken for the subjects to respond to counsellors and non-counsellors. Any differences found in our results are due to chance.

Note: We have used the same data for all the related samples tests (Sign Test, Wilcoxon Test and Related t-Test). This enables us to demonstrate the differences between the rough-and-ready Sign Test and the more sophisticated Wilcoxon Test. The Sign test has found this data not significant, whereas the more powerful Wilcoxon Test which begins looking at the size of the differences through its use of ranks, finds this data significant, (see page 68).

The Wilcoxon Signed Ranks Test

When to use the Wilcoxon Test.

The Wilcoxon Test is designed to be used with the data drawn from experiments using either a repeated measures or matched pairs design. Whilst it is more powerful than the Sign Test, because it actually takes into account the size of the differences between the two conditions, it is still a non-parametric test and therefore places less demands on the type of data and the population from which it is obtained. A t-test for related samples requires that data is interval or ratio, the Wilcoxon Test, however, may be used with ordinal data; the basic requirement of the test being that scores by each subject can be ranked in comparison to all other subjects, thus it is important that the subjects can score higher or lower than other subjects on whatever variable is being measured. The test can be used instead of a t-test, but the usual reasons for choosing the Wilcoxon Test are to avoid having to meet the requirements of a t-test, or simply because it is easier (or shorter) to calculate.

What the test does

The reasoning behind this test is quite simple. In doing the test, what is being analysed are the differences between the scores of each subject in Condition A and Condition B. If there is a significant difference, we would expect that most subjects will tend to de better in one of the conditions than the other; so that when the differences are calculated the majority of the differences will tend to be positive if the subjects have tended to perform better in Condition A, or negative if subjects have tended to perform better in Condition B. If there is no significant difference, some subjects will have performed better in Condition A and others will have performed better in Condition B. Thus when the differences are analysed there will be a mixture of both positive and negative differences.

To discover whether or not this is the case, the differences between the scores in the two conditions are ranked, and the number of positive and negative differences are counted. Taking whichever occurs the least, the ranks for these differences are added together; if the resulting figure is small, this suggests that any differences that disagree with the main trend are small, and that the usual result is for the differences between the two conditions of the experiment to follow a pattern; suggesting that there is a significant difference. If however, the sum of the least frequent differences is large, this suggests that there is no overall pattern to performance by the subjects, that some subjects do perform better in one condition, and that other subjects perform better in the other condition; thus there is no significant difference.

Calculating the Wilcoxon Test

STEP 1: Draw a simple table (see page 67) and enter all the scores from Condition A in the first column and all the scores from Condition B in the second. Scores for each subject should lie next to each other in the two columns.

STEP 2: For each subject (each pair of scores), subtract the scores in Condition B from the scores in Condition A (A - B) to find the difference (referred to as d). Enter these in the column marked d.

STEP 3: Rank all the difference scores from the smallest (rank 1) to the highest (rank N). At this stage it does not matter whether the scores are negative or positive; a score of 4 would be smaller than a score of -6.

Note : If there are any subjects who have scored exactly the same in both conditions and therefore have a difference score of 0, these should be left out of the calculations from this point.

STEP 4: Count up the number of cases where the difference between the scores is positive, and the number of cases where the difference between the scores is negative. Select whichever of these happens the least often, and add together all the ranks for cases where this occurs. Call the figure you arrive at T. This is your **obtained value**.

STEP 5: Count the number of subjects whose scores have been included in the calculation (don't include the subjects who had no difference between the scores in the two conditions). Call this number N.

STEP 6: Decide on the level of significance (this will depend on whether your test is one-tailed or two-tailed).

STEP 7: Look up the critical value for your test from the table on page 106. This will depend on N (number of subjects) and the significance level decided upon.

STEP 8: Compare the obtained value of T to the critical value from the table. If the obtained value is less than or equal to the critical value reject the null hypothesis and accept the alternate (experimental) hypothesis.

Worked Example
The same data is used as for the worked example of the Sign Test. *STEPS 1 to 3* have been conducted on the table below.

SUBJECT	SCORES IN CONDITION A	SCORES IN CONDITION B	DIFFERENCE (A - B) d	RANKED DIFFERENCES
1	17	12	5	5.5
2	19	15	4	4
3	21	15	6	7
4	17	19	-2	2
5	17	9	8	8
6	25	25	0	omitted
7	15	10	5	5.5
8	32	17	15	11
9	20	17	3	3
10	22	12	10	9
11	17	6	11	10
12	15	16	-1	1

STEP 4: There are 9 cases where the differences are positive (score in Condition A is higher than score in Condition B) and 2 cases where the difference is negative, therefore negative is the least occurring sign.

The ranks for the scores of the least occurring sign are 1 and 2. (See last two columns, rank 1 has a difference of -1 and rank 2 has a difference of -2)

Obtained value $T = 1 + 2 = 3$
$T = 3$

STEP 5: Find   N (number of relevant scores)
$N = 11$
Note: *There are 12 subjects, but 1 subject (subject 6) has scored the same in both conditions, therefore has been omitted from the calculation, this leaves 11 subjects on whom the calculation is based.*

STEP 6: Significance level = 5% ($p \leq 0.05$)
This is the usual significance level.

STEP 7: The table on page 106 shows that, when $N = 11$ and the significance level is 5% ($p \leq 0.05$) for a two-tailed hypothesis, the **critical value** is 10.

STEP 8: The **obtained value** of T (3) is less than the **critical value** found in the table (10). Therefore the null hypothesis can be rejected, and the experimental hypothesis accepted. The probability is that the difference between the scores in the two conditions is not due to chance, i.e. that the difference is significant. We can this time conclude that there is a difference between response times to counsellors and non-counsellors. This is in contrast to the findings of the Sign Test using the same data.

t-Test for Related Samples
(Related t-Test)

When to use the Related t-Test.

The t-test is a parametric test for use with data obtained using a repeated measures or matched pairs design. As a parametric test more restrictions are placed on the type and nature of the data on which the test can be conducted. As the test makes greater mathematical use of the data than either the Wilcoxon or Sign tests, the level of data required is interval or ratio. Additionally, the data from both conditions of the experiment should be normally distributed, and the variance of the two sets of data should be equal.

Having said the above, it is worth repeating that the t-test is a robust test; the assumptions about the distribution of the variances can be slightly abused without significant loss of the test's power to detect a significant difference where one exists.

What the Related t-Test Does

The t-test calculation is based on the actual difference in scores between the two conditions (rather than the differences in the ranked performance used by the Wilcoxon test). The test looks at the size of the average difference between the two conditions. If the difference between the performances in the two conditions is significant, then the differences will tend to be relatively large.

The test also checks that the average difference between the two sets of scores is the product of relatively consistent differences between the two conditions rather than a few subjects producing large differences whilst the rest of the subjects show little or no difference in performance. Additionally, the test confirms that the differences between the conditions are in a consistent direction (i.e. that subjects tend to perform better in Condition A than Condition B or vice versa). This is important because it could be that the average difference between the two conditions is relatively large, but that this is because some subjects perform much better on Condition A than Condition B, but the other subjects show the reverse pattern. The difference can only be considered significant if it is the result of a consistent pattern of differences.

Calculating the Related t-Test

STEP 1: Draw a simple table in which you enter all the scores from Condition A in one column and all the scores from Condition B in a second. Scores for each subject should lie next to each other in the two columns, (see p72)

STEP 2: For each subject i.e. each pair of scores, subtract the scores from Condition B from Condition A (A - B) to find the difference (referred to as d). Enter these in the column marked d.

STEP 3: Add up all the d (difference) scores to find Σd .
Note: Remember that any minus figures should be deducted from the total rather than added to it. The easiest way to do this is to add up all the positive scores and then subtract any remaining negative scores.

STEP 4: Divide the figure obtained in *STEP 3* (Σd) by the number of subjects (n). This gives the mean difference score ($\overline{d}$).

STEP 5: Square each d score and enter these in the final column (conveniently marked d^2).

STEP 6: Add up all the scores in the final column to find the total of the squared differences; this figure is Σd^2 .

The figures that have been calculated so far are:

Σd The sum of all the difference scores
$\overline{d}$ The mean of all the difference scores.
Σd^2 The sum of all the squared differences.
n   The number of subjects.

STEP 7: Substitute the above figures in the following formula and calculate the obtained value *t*

$$t = \overline{d} \Big/ \sqrt{\frac{\sum d^2 - (\sum d)^2/n}{n\,(n-1)}}$$

This looks complicated, but if followed step by step is simply time consuming.

i) Square $\sum d$ (the sum of all the difference scores).
In the formula this is shown as $(\sum d)^2$

ii) Divide the figure you obtained from the last stage by n (the number of subjects).
In the formula this is shown as $(\sum d)^2/n$

iii) Subtract the figure you have just calculated from $\sum d^2$ (the sum of all the squared differences)
In the formula this is shown as $\sum d^2 - (\sum d)^2/n$

iv) Subtract 1 from n (number of subjects)

v) Multiply the number you have just worked out by n (number of subjects)
In the formula this is shown as n (n - 1)

vi) Divide the figure you obtained in stage iii by the number you obtained in stage v
In the formula this is shown as $\dfrac{\sum d^2 - (\sum d)^2/n}{n\,(n-1)}$

vii) Find the square root of the number you have just obtained. (Generally this is done by pressing the key marked $\sqrt{\ }$ on your calculator).

In the formula this is shown as
$$\sqrt{\frac{\sum d^2 - (\sum d)^2/n}{n\,(n-1)}}$$

viii) Divide d (mean of the differences) by the figure you obtained in stage vii. This gives you *t*; your *obtained value*.

This is the formula shown at the beginning of *STEP 7*

STEP 8: Find the degrees of freedom (df) by subtracting 1 from the number of subjects:
$$df = n - 1$$

STEP 9: Decide on the significance level. This will usually be 5% ($p \leq 0.05$).

STEP 10: Using the table of critical values of *t* on page 104, find the **critical value** of *t*. This will depend on both degrees of freedom and the level of significance.

STEP 11: If the **obtained value** of *t* is more than or equal to the **critical value**, the null hypothesis can be rejected; i.e. the difference between the two sets of scores is significant.

Worked Example

SUBJ-ECT	SCORES IN CONDITION A	SCORES IN CONDITION B	DIFFERENCE (A - B) d	SQUARED DIFFERENCES d^2
1	17	12	5	25
2	19	15	4	16
3	21	15	6	36
4	17	19	-2	4
5	17	9	8	64
6	25	25	0	0
7	15	10	5	25
8	32	17	15	225
9	20	17	3	9
10	22	12	10	100
11	17	6	11	121
12	15	16	-1	1
			$\Sigma d = 64$	$\Sigma d^2 = 626$

Note: The same data is used in this example as is used in the Sign Test and Wilcoxon Test Worked Example

STEPS 1 and *2* have been conducted on the table.

STEP 3: The figures in the d column are added to give Σd.
Note: the minus figures (-2 and -3) have been deducted from the total rather than added to it (see bottom of the table page72).

STEP 4: The Σd figure obtained in the previous step is divided by n (n = 12) to give $\bar{d}$ (the mean of the differences).

$$\bar{d} = \frac{\Sigma d}{n} = \frac{64}{12} = 5.33$$

STEP 5: Square each d score and enter these in the final column. This has been done on the table.

STEP 6: All the scores in the final column are added to give Σd^2

So far, the following values have been calculated:

Σd	=	64	The sum of all the difference scores.
$\bar{d}$	=	5.33	The mean of all the difference scores.
Σd^2	=	626	The sum of all the squared differences.
n	=	12	The number of subjects.

STEP 7: Substitute the above figures in the following formula and calculate the obtained value *t*.

$$t = d \bigg/ \sqrt{\frac{\Sigma d^2 - (\Sigma d)^2/n}{n(n-1)}}$$

i) Square Σd to get $(\Sigma d)^2$ as shown in the formula.
   $64 \times 64 = 4096$

ii) To get $(\Sigma d)^2/n$ divide the figure you obtained in stage i by n (number of subjects).

$$\frac{4096}{12} = 341.33$$

iii) Calculate $\Sigma d^2 - (\Sigma d)^2/n$ by subtracting the figure you have obtained in stage ii from Σd^2 (the sum of all the squared differences).

$$626 - 341.33 = 284.67$$

iv) Subtract 1 from n (number of subjects)

$$(n - 1) = 12 - 1 = 11$$

v) Multiply the number you have just worked out in stage iv by n (number of subjects).

$$n(n - 1) = 12 \times 11 = 132$$

vi) Now divide the figure you obtained in stage iii by the number you obtained in stage v to get

$$\frac{\Sigma d^2 - (\Sigma d)^2/n}{n(n-1)} = \frac{284.33}{132} = 2.1565909$$

vii) Find the square root of the number you have just obtained

$$\sqrt{2.1565909} = 1.4685335$$

viii) Divide d (mean of the differences) by the figure you have just obtained in stage vii.
This gives you t; your **obtained value**.

$$t = \frac{5.33}{1.685335} = 3.6294711$$

STEP 8 : Calculate the degrees of freedom

$$df = n - 1 = 12 - 1 = 11$$
$$df = 11$$

STEP 9 : Significance level = 5% (p ≤ 0.05) for a two-tailed test.

STEP 10 : From the table of critical values of *t* on page 104, the **critical value** of *t* with 11 df = 2.201

STEP 11 : As the **obtained value** of *t* (*t* = 3.6294711) is greater than the **critical value** of *t* (*t* = 2.201), the null hypothesis can be rejected; the difference between the scores in the two conditions is significant.

Again we can conclude that there is a significant difference between the response times to a counsellor compared to a non-counsellor. However, because we chose a two-tailed hypothesis, we cannot comment on the significance of the direction of the difference, i.e. whether responses were quicker to the counsellor or non-counsellor.

Spearman's Rank Order Correlation Coefficient

When to use Spearman's Rank Test

As with the other correlation coefficients, Spearman's is calculated when we wish to know the degree and type of any relationship between two variables rather than whether one variable has had an effect on the other.

The Spearman's test is a non-parametric test for correlation. It requires at least ordinal data from each of the variables being measured; i.e. subjects should be able to score higher or lower than each other on each of the variables being measured.

The Spearman's test can be performed on both interval or ratio data, but the main reason for this, assuming that the data meets the other requirements of a parametric test, is that it is much simpler to calculate than the Pearson's Product Moment, which is the parametric alternative.

What the Spearman's Rank does

Rather than looking at the differences between the actual (and the mean) scores (which is what a parametric test would do), the Spearman's test looks at the differences between the ranks. Each subject's score on each of the variables is ranked, and the difference between these is calculated. If the differences are small, this would indicate that those subjects who were ranked highly on the first variable were also ranked highly on the other variable, and those who were ranked low on the first variable were also ranked low on the other variable. This would be indicative of a positive correlation; the smaller the differences in the ranks, the greater the relationship and the higher the correlation. Conversely, if the differences in the ranks are large, this would indicate that those subjects ranked high on the first variable tend to be ranked low on the other variable (and vice versa). This would produce a negative correlation, the greater the difference in the ranks, the stronger the relationship. Where no pattern emerges in the relationship between ranks awarded to subjects on the two variables, a low or non-significant relationship emerges.

Calculating the Spearman's Rank

STEP 1: Construct a table including the same headings as the one below. The depth of the table will obviously depend on the number of subjects you have, but the number of columns is always the same.

SUBJECT	SCORE ON VARIABLE X	SCORE ON VARIABLE Y	RANK OF VARIABLE X	RANK OF VARIABLE Y	DIFFER-ENCE d	DIFFER-ENCE SQUARED d^2
1 2 3 etc.						

STEP 2: Insert the scores on the first variable into the second column and those of the second variable into the third. We now refer to these as Variable X and Variable Y. (These are just mathematical 'names' - because we have to call them something.)

STEP 3: In the fourth column (headed RANK OF VARIABLE X) rank all the scores on the first variable from the lowest to the highest. The lowest score will have rank 1, highest score will have rank n, which will depend on how many subjects you have used.

Repeat this procedure for the other set of scores, placing the ranks in the fifth column (headed RANK OF VARIABLE Y).

Note: *Be careful when you do this. Another way of putting the instruction would be to say, rank the scores from worst to best. For example, if you were ranking the scores on a maths test, then ranking from lowest to highest would take you from worst to best.*
BUT, if you were ranking the times taken to complete the test, the lowest score is in fact the best score, so in this case you would rank from highest (worst) to lowest (best).

STEP 4: Find the difference between the ranks for each individual subject. This is done by subtracting the ranks for Variable Y from the ranks for Variable X, and enter this in the 6th column, which is headed DIFFERENCE.

> For example, Subject 1 has a rank of 2 for the first variable and a rank of 7 from the second variable.
>
> So 2 - 7 = -5

If you do have a minus figure, keep the minus sign in the table for the time being, we shall be getting rid of it shortly.

STEP 5: Square each of the difference scores and insert these in the last column.

Note : To square the number simply multiply it by itself. So, if you want to square the number 5, you multiply 5 x 5 = 25.
If your score is -5 and you multiply it by itself   -5 x -5 = 25.
(The same is true of any minus number, multiplying minus signs together always gives a plus.) Also note that 0 x 0 = 0.

STEP 6: Add up all the scores in the last column.

This gives the figure $\sum d^2$ (Sum of the squared differences).

STEP 7: Count the number of subjects (call this N).

STEP 8: Calculate the correlation coefficient (called r) using the following formula

$$r = \frac{6\sum d^2}{N(N^2-1)}$$

i) Multiply $\sum d^2$ by 6.

ii) Square your N value, and then subtract 1.

iii) Multiply the figure you have just obtained in stage ii by N.

iv) Divide the figure you obtained in stage i by the figure you obtained in stage iii.

v) Subtract the figure you obtained in stage iv from 1.
This gives us our correlation coefficient.

Note: If the figure is larger than 1, you will get a minus figure. This is OK as it indicates that you have a negative correlation; so leave the minus figure as it stands.

STEP 9: Find the **critical value** using the table of values on page 107. This will depend on N (number of subjects) and the significance level chosen (normally $p \leq 0.05$).

If the **obtained value** of r (your correlation coefficient) is equal to or more than the **critical value**, reject the null hypothesis; the relation between the two variables is significant.
Note : You will need to know whether your hypothesis is one-tailed (i.e. you have predicted the type of relationship - positive or negative),or two-tailed in order to find the correct critical value. (See Sanders and Liptrot 1993, p121)

Worked Example

Imagine you want to look at the relationship between counselling aptitude and creativity. You have selected 10 subjects, and given each of them a counselling aptitude test and a creativity test. We will now look to see if there is a correlation between the two sets of scores. If you are not familiar with the procedures for collecting data for correlations, read Sanders and Liptrot (1993), p116-122.

STEPS 1 - 5 are completed on the table as follows:
STEP 1: Construct a table as shown on page 80.

STEP 2: Insert the scores on the first variable into the second column and insert the scores on the other variable into the third column.

STEP 3: In the fourth column (RANK OF VARIABLE X) rank all the scores on the first variable from lowest to highest. Repeat this procedure for the other set of scores, placing the ranks in the 5th column (RANK OF VARIABLE Y).

SUBJECT	SCORE ON VARIABLE X	SCORE ON VARIABLE Y	RANK OF VARIABLE X	RANK OF VARIABLE Y	DIFFER-ENCE d	DIFFER-ENCE SQUARED d^2
1	100	46	2	7	-5	25
2	122	37	6	5	1	1
3	113	48	4	8	-4	16
4	145	29	10	2	8	64
5	98	72	1	10	-9	81
6	122	38	6	6	0	0
7	133	32	8	3	5	25
8	140	19	9	1	8	64
9	122	36	6	4	2	4
10	106	60	3	9	-6	36

$$\sum d^2 = 316$$

STEP 4: Find the difference between the ranks for each individual subject. (See table above.)

STEP 5: Square each of the difference scores, and insert these in the last column. (See table above.)

STEP 6: $\sum d^2$ = 316 (Sum of the squared differences, see table above.).

STEP 7: N = 10 (number of subjects).

STEP 8: Calculate the correlation coefficient r using the following formula:

$$r = \frac{6\sum d^2}{N(N^2-1)}$$

i) Add all the scores in the final column and multiply by 6:   6 x 316 = 1896

ii) Find the square of N : 10 x 10 = 100
Then subtract 1 : 100 - 1 = 99

iii) Multiply the figure you have just obtained by N :
99 x 10 = 990

iv) Divide the figure you obtained in stage i by the
figure you obtained in stage iii : $\frac{1896}{990}$ = 1.915

v) Subtract the figure obtained in stage iv from 1:
1 - 1.915 = -0.915
This gives us the correlation coefficient r = - 0.915

This is the **obtained value**.

*Note : The figure obtained is a negative figure, indicating that the
correlation is negative. This means that as one variable increases
the other decreases, (see Sanders and Liptrot 1993, p116-122).*

STEP 9 : Find the **critical value** using the table of critical values
of r on page 107. This will depend on N and significance level:

N = 10
Significance p ≤ 0.05
Critical value = 0.65

As the **obtained value** of r is greater that the **critical value**, we
reject the null hypothesis; the relationship between the two variables
is significant.

Since the correlation is negative we can conclude that as counselling
aptitude increases, creativity decreases (and vice versa).

Pearson's Product Moment
Correlation Coefficient

When to use the Pearson's Product Moment Test

The Pearson's Product Moment test is the parametric alternative to the Spearman's Rank Correlation Coefficient. It should be used when looking for a significant relationship (correlation) between two variables. However, the data should meet the requirements of a parametric test described on page 7.

What the Pearson's Product Moment Test does.

As with other parametric tests, Pearson's test is calculated using the raw data rather than converting the scores to ranks. It is this use of the actual scores that gives the test its greater power and sensitivity compared to the non-parametric equivalent. The basis of the test is as follows:

The correlation coefficient depends on calculating the degree to which the scores of each subject differ from the mean on each of the two variables. (In the equation this is called DXDY.) The larger this figure is for a subject, the greater the difference between their two scores and their means. If the figure is a negative figure, this indicates that their score is higher than the mean on one variable, and lower than the mean on the other variable. If this is the case for a large number of the subjects, the result will be a negative correlation. The total of these scores will reflect this.

If there is a consistent pattern of scores by subjects on the two variables, the total of the DXDY scores will be relatively high (either positive or negative), but when there is no pattern to subjects performances on the two variables, the positive and negative DXDY scores will cancel each other out, and there will be a relatively low score. The DXDY total is divided by the square root of (ΣDX^2) (ΣDY^2). This figure represents a combination of the standard deviations of scores on the two variables. If the pattern of the DXDY scores is inconsistent, this will produce a low score indicating a low correlation, but when there is a consistent pattern to subjects performances (relatively high DXDY total) this will produce a high correlation coefficient.

Note : Using the same data, the Spearman's Rank Correlation Coefficient produced a slightly higher coefficient (-0.915). This is because the two tests make use of the data in different ways. See the section on parametric and non-parametric tests on page 5.

Calculating the Pearson's Product Moment Test

STEP 1 : Construct a table using the headings shown below.

sub-ject	score on variable X	DX score $(X-\bar{X})$	DX² score	score on variable Y	DY score $(Y-\bar{Y})$	DY² score	DXDY score
1 2 3 etc.							
	ΣDX^2				ΣDY^2		
						$\Sigma DXDY$	

STEP 2 : Enter each subject's score on the first variable (Variable X) in the second column of the table.

STEP 3 : Find the mean of the scores by adding all the scores together and dividing by the number of the scores.
Call this figure $\bar{X}$

STEP 4 : Subtract the mean score $\bar{X}$ from each of the scores in column 2. Enter each of these difference scores in the third column (DX).

Note: Remember to leave in any minus signs as these will be important later.

STEP 5 : Square each of the DX scores and enter these squared DX scores in the fourth column of the table (DX^2)

STEP 6 : Add up all the scores in the DX^2 column.
    Call this figure ΣDX^2

STEP 7 : Enter each subject's score on the second variable (Variable Y) in the fifth column of the table.

STEP 8 : Find the mean of the Y scores by adding all the scores together and dividing by the number of scores.
    Call this figure $\overline{Y}$

STEP 9 : Subtract the mean score $\overline{Y}$ from each of the Y scores in column 5. Enter each of these difference scores in the sixth column (DY).
Note: *Remember to leave in any minus signs as these will be important later.*

STEP 10 : Square each of the DY scores and enter these DY^2 scores in the seventh column of the table (DY^2).

STEP 11 : Add up all the scores in the DY^2 column.
    Call this figure ΣDY^2

STEP 12 : For each subject, multiply the DX scores and the DY scores together. Place these scores in the final column (DXDY). The DX and DY scores are in the third and sixth columns.
Note : *Remember to include any minus signs when multiplying; a plus times a minus will produce a minus figure, and a minus times a minus will produce a plus; this is important.*

STEP 13 : Add up all the scores in the DXDY column.
    Call this figure ΣDXDY
Note : *It should be remembered that some of the scores may have minus signs in front of them; these should be taken into account.*

The best way to do this is to add up all the scores with no minus sign, and then subtract all the scores that do have a minus sign. It may be that you will end up with a minus figure. All this means is that you will have a negative correlation.

You should now have the following values:

ΣDX^2 $\qquad\qquad$ ΣDY^2 $\qquad\qquad$ $\Sigma DXDY$

STEP 14: Calculate the correlation coefficient (r) by the following stages.

i) Multiply ΣDX^2 by ΣDY^2

ii) Find the square root of the figure you have just obtained in stage i.

iii) Divide $\Sigma DXDY$ by the number obtained in stage ii. This gives your correlation coefficient r.

$$ r = \frac{\Sigma DXDY}{\sqrt{(\Sigma DX^2)(\Sigma DY^2)}} $$

STEP 15: Calculate the degrees of freedom by subtracting 2 from N (N-2), when N is the number of subjects.

STEP 16: Select the significance level (usually $p \leq 0.05$).

STEP 17: Use the table on page 108 to find the **critical value**. This will depend on the number of subjects (N) and the significance level.

STEP 18: Compare the **obtained value** of r (the correlation Coefficient obtained in *STEP 14* stage iii with the **critical value** shown in the table. If the obtained value of r is larger than or equal to the critical value, reject the null hypothesis. The relationship is significant. **Note** : *It does not matter if the final correlation coefficient has a minus figure in front of it (a negative correlation). It just matters whether the obtained value of the correlation coefficient is larger than the critical value or not.*

Worked Example

During counselling sessions, 2 variables were measured. Variable X is the amount of time in seconds that subjects made eye contact with the counsellor. Variable Y is the amount of time in seconds that the counsellors spent looking at the client. We wish to see if there is a significant relationship between these two variables. If you are not familiar with the procedures for collecting data for correlations, read Sanders and Liptrot 1993, p116-122.

Note : This example and data is exactly the same as that for the Spearman's Rank Correlation Coefficient. It will be interesting to see the degree of similarity in the correlation coefficients produced by the two tests.

sub-ject	score on variable X	DX score (X-X)	DX² score	score on variable Y	DY score (Y-Y)	DY² score	DXDY score
1	100	-20.1	404.01	46	4.3	18.49	-86.43
2	122	1.9	3.61	37	-4.7	22.09	-8.93
3	113	-7.1	50.41	48	6.3	39.69	-44.73
4	145	24.9	620.01	29	-12.7	161.29	-316.23
5	98	-22.1	488.41	72	30.3	918.09	-669.63
6	122	1.9	3.61	38	-3.7	13.69	-7.03
7	133	12.9	166.41	32	-9.7	94.09	-125.13
8	140	19.9	396.01	19	-22.7	515.29	-451.73
9	122	1.9	3.61	36	-5.7	32.49	-10.83
10	106	-14.1	198.81	60	18.3	334.89	-258.03

$$\Sigma DX^2 \quad 2331.29 \qquad \Sigma DY^2 \quad 2150.1$$

$$\Sigma DXDY \quad -1978.7$$

STEPS 1 and *2* performed in the table above.

STEP 3: Calculate the mean of the scores on variable X

$$\overline{X} \ = \ 120.1$$

STEP 4: For each subject subtract $\overline{X}$ from the X variable score.
e.g. for subject 1: score = 100, mean = 120.1
 DX = score - mean = 100 - 120.1 = -20.1 (See table col. 3.)

STEP 5: Square each DX score obtained in *STEP 4*.
e.g. for subject 1: DX = -20.1, so DX^2 = 404.01 (See table col . 4.)

STEP 6: Add up all the scores in the DX column:
ΣDX^2 = 2331.29 (sum of all DX^2 scores)

STEP 7: Enter each subject's score on Variable Y into column 5 in
the table.

STEP 8: Calculate the mean of the scores on VariableY
$\qquad \overline{Y} = 41.7$

STEP 9: For each subject subtract $\overline{Y}$ from the Y variable score.
e.g. for subject 1: score = 46, mean = 41.7
DY = score - mean = 46 - 41.7 = 4.3 (See table col. 6.)

STEP 10: Square each DY score (obtained in *STEP 9*).
e.g. for subject 1: DY = 4.3, so DY^2 = 18.49 (See table col. 4.)

STEP 11: Add up all the scores in the DY column:
$\qquad \Sigma$DY^2 = 2150.1 (sum of all DY^2 scores).

STEP 12: For each subject multiply the DX and the DY scores
together,
e.g. for student 1: DX score = - 20.1, DY score = 4.3
DXDY = - 20.1 x 4.3 = - 86.43 (enter into the last column).

STEP 13: Add up the scores in the DXDY column:
$\qquad \Sigma$DXDY = - 1978.7

Now we have : $\qquad \Sigma$DX^2 = 2331.29
$\qquad\qquad\qquad\quad \Sigma$DY^2 = 2150.1
$\qquad\qquad\qquad\quad \Sigma$DXDY = -1978.7

STEP 14: Calculate correlation coefficient (r).
    i) Multiply $\sum DX^2$ by $\sum DY^2$ - this is $(\sum DX^2)(\sum DY^2)$

$$2331.29 \ x \ 2150.1 = 5012506.6$$

ii) Find the square root of 5012506.6

$$\sqrt{5012506.6} = 2238.8627$$

This is $\sqrt{(\sum DX^2)(\sum DY^2)}$

iii) Calculate r = $\sum DXDY$ divided by the number obtained in stage ii.

$$r = \frac{-1978.7}{2238.8627} = -0.884 \ \text{(rounded to three decimal places)}$$

STEP 15: Degrees of freedom = (N-2) = (10 -2) = 8

STEP 16 : Significance level $p \le 0.05$ (usual significant level).

STEP 17: From table of critical values of Pearsons' r on page 108, **critical value** = 0.632 (when df = 8 and p $\le$ 0.05)

STEP 18: As the **obtained value** of r (-0.884) is larger than the **critical value** (0.632), the null hypothesis can be rejected. The relationship between the two variables is significant.

This means that in our example there is a significant negative correlation between the amount of time the counsellor looks at the client and the amount of time the client looks at the counsellor. The fact that the relationship is negative means that the **more** the counsellor looks at the client, the **less** the client looks at the counsellor.

The One-Way Analysis of Variance (ANOVA)

When to use the One-Way ANOVA

With the exception of the Chi-squared test, all the tests of difference in this book look at situations where we are testing differences between two groups. In real-life research however, even on a small scale, we are often interested in what happens in more than two groups. For example, we may want to compare five branches of a voluntary counselling service to see if there was any difference in the length of time they keep their volunteers. This is where *Analyses of Variance* come in, they allow us to look at three, four, indeed any number of groups of data at once. ANOVA's were never really intended to be used with large numbers of groups. Realistically around five or six groups is reasonable and you will find that even then, the calculations can be a bit of a handful.

The ANOVA introduced here is called the One-Way ANOVA because it deals with only one factor in the data. In our example above the factor in question is that the volunteers measured for length of service come from different branches. We could introduce another factor and look at the gender of the volunteers as well. We would use a Two-Way ANOVA for this. We could then tell if women volunteers stay longer than men volunteers, whether length of service depends which branch you belong to, and finally whether there is any interaction between these two factors. This is, however a much more complex, time consuming calculation and calls for a great deal more explanation than is appropriate at this level.

So, a One-Way ANOVA is to be used when we are interested in looking at differences between more than two groups.

It is a parametric test, so it makes the usual assumptions about the population parameters (see page 7). Also, as with other parametric tests, it is robust, i.e. if the sample sizes are equal, violation of assumptions 1 and 2 below will not destroy the integrity of the test. The measurements, however, must always be independent (see 3 below). The ANOVA makes the following assumptions about the data:

1. The individual scores in each group should be randomly selected from normally distributed populations.

2. The variance of each group should be roughly equal.

3. The samples of scores in each group should be independent. That is to say that each sample should be from a different source, i.e. it is essentially an independent groups test. (See Sanders and Liptrot 1993, p112-113.)

What the One-Way ANOVA does.

The name implies (incorrectly) that the test compares the variances of the samples of scores. In fact it compares sample means rather like a t-test. It compares the sample means to each other and to the overall mean of all the scores mixed together. It does this by calculating the sum of squares of the data in three different ways: the sum of squares is a calculation made on the way to working out the variance (see Sanders and Liptrot 1993, p57-58).

The ANOVA works out the sum of the squares between the groups, the sum of the squares within each group and the sum of the squares of all of the scores together. This information on its own is useful and can then put these sums of squares in a summary table, but we take the analysis one stage further by computing an F-Ratio or F-Test on these sums of squares to see if they show a significant effect, i.e. differences between the sums of squares that are unlikely to have occurred by chance.

ANOVA's have two advantages over t- tests (which you could use in similar circumstances, but with unsatisfactory and unanalysable results):

1. They cut down the number and complexity of the calculations. This saves time and reduces the possibility of computational errors. For example, we may want to compare five branches of a voluntary

counselling service to see if there was any difference in the length of time they keep their volunteers. We could use t-tests to compare the services but t-tests only compare the means of two groups at a time. This would mean doing ten t-tests in order to compare all five branches with each other.

2. They allow us to take into account sub-samples which may exist in a set. Sub-samples are known to interact and one-way ANOVA's do not ignore this interaction.

Finally, the F-Ratio or F-Test at the end of the ANOVA can be used separately to compare any variances in pairs. It is occasionally used, for example, to see whether the variances in two groups are equal before doing a t-test.

Calculation of the One-Way ANOVA

STEP 1: Draw a table with the headings shown below depending upon the number of groups you are working with. The table drawn below is for three groups of data:

Group A X	Group B X	Group C X	Group A squared X^2	Group B squared X^2	Group C squared X^2

$\Sigma XA=$ $\quad \Sigma XB=$ $\quad \Sigma XC=$ $\quad \Sigma XA^2=$ $\quad \Sigma XB^2=$ $\quad \Sigma XC^2=$

$\Sigma X=$ $\qquad\qquad\qquad\qquad\qquad \Sigma X^2=$

$\overline{XA}=$ $\quad\quad \overline{XB}=$ $\quad\quad \overline{XC}=$

$\overline{X}_{tot}=$ $\qquad\qquad\qquad\qquad N = NA + NB + NC =$

STEP 2: Write the scores from the first group in the first column, the second group in the second column, third group third column, etc.
Note: It doesn't matter what order you put the groups in as far as the maths goes. It may, however, make sense for you to put them in a particular logical order that makes sense in your study.

STEP 3: Square each score from column 1 and put it in column 4, square each score from column 2 and put it in column 5, the squares of the third group go in column 6, etc.

STEP 4: Work out ΣXA by adding up the scores in column 1 and putting the total at the bottom of the column next to the ΣXA symbol. Work out ΣXB and ΣXC in the same way, putting the totals next to the appropriate symbols.

STEP 5: Work out ΣXA^2 by adding up the squared scores in column 4 and putting the total at the bottom of the column next to the ΣXA^2 symbol. Work out ΣXB^2 and ΣXC^2 in the same way, putting the totals next to the appropriate symbols.

STEP 6: Work out ΣX by adding up the column totals at the bottom of columns 1, 2 and 3:
$$\Sigma X = \Sigma XA + \Sigma XB + \Sigma XC$$
and put the answer next to the ΣX symbol.

STEP 7: Work out ΣX^2 by adding up the totals of the squares scores at the bottom of columns 4, 5 and 6:
$$\Sigma X^2 = \Sigma XA^2 + \Sigma XB^2 + \Sigma XC^2$$
and put the answer next to the ΣX^2 symbol.

STEP 8: Work out the mean of each group of scores by dividing the totals obtained in STEP 4 and dividing by the number of scores in each group NA, NB, and NC:

Example: $\overline{XA} = \dfrac{\Sigma XA}{NA}$ put the answer next to the XA symbol.

Work out $\overline{XB}$ and $\overline{XC}$ in the same way, putting the means next to the appropriate symbols.

STEP 9: Work out the mean of all of the scores in all of the groups by adding together the mean of each group and dividing by the number of groups (the number of groups is referred to as 'k'):

$$X_{tot} = \dfrac{XA + XB + XC}{k}$$ put the answer next to the X_{tot} symbol.

Note: You have now completed the table. The remaining calculations simply make use of the calculations you have completed so far. In terms of time, we're about half way through the full calculation.

STEP 10: Work out the **Total Sum-of-Squares** by substituting some of the figures calculated above (bottom of table on page 91) in the following equation:

$$SS_T = \Sigma X^2 - \frac{(\Sigma X)^2}{N}$$

STEP 11: Work out the Between Sum-of-Squares by substituting more of the figures calculated above (bottom of table on page 91) in the following equation:

$$SS_B = \left(\frac{(\Sigma XA)^2}{NA} + \frac{(\Sigma XB)^2}{NB} + \frac{(\Sigma XC)^2}{NC} \right) - \frac{(\Sigma X_T)^2}{N}$$

Note: This is a shorthand way of calculating the 'between sum-of-squares and is mathematically not quite as accurate as a much more long-winded but more 'correct' method. It is accurate within one decimal place and therefore will not corrupt your overall conclusions.

STEP 12: Calculate the Within Sum-of Squares by finding the sum-of squares for each group as follows:

Example for group A: $SS_{GA} = \Sigma XA^2 - \frac{(\Sigma XA)^2}{NA}$

Follow the same procedure for each group. Then add the SS's for each group together to get the Within Sum-of-Squares.

$SS_W = SS_{GA} + SS_{GB} + SS_{GC}$ ....depending on the number of groups in your study.

Note: It will soon become obvious that you don't actually have to do this bit, but in most books it's recommended as a computational check. In other words its a check against making a silly mistake in your calculations so far. This may seem like a waste of time, but when you are squaring such big numbers, a little mistake soon becomes a little mistake squared which is then a very big mistake and can throw your calculations out wildly. If you work all of your

SS's out, you will at least know whether you have followed the calculations through correctly.

STEP 13: This is the computational check: the **Within Sum-of-Squares** added to the **Between Sum-of-Squares** should equal the **Total Sum-of-Squares**. It follows then that the **Within Sum-of-Squares** can be obtained directly by subtracting the **Between Sum-of-Squares** from the **Total Sum-of-Squares**, both of which we've already worked out.

$$SS_T = SS_B + SS_W \quad (\text{or } SS_W = SS_T - SS_B)$$

STEP 14: Work out the degrees of freedom for the three Sums-of-Squares as follows:
    df for Total SS = total number of scores minus 1 = N - 1
    df for Between SS = number of groups minus 1 = k - 1
    df for Within SS = [number of scores in group A minus 1 added to the number of scores in group B minus 1 added to the number of scores in group C minus 1] = (NA - 1) + (NB - 1) + (NC - 1)

STEP 15: Calculate the Mean Square values for the source of variance within groups and the source of variance between groups by dividing each of the sums of squares by their respective degrees of freedom:

Between Groups Mean Square   = $\dfrac{\text{Between Groups SS}}{\text{Between Groups df}}$

Within Groups Mean Square   = $\dfrac{\text{Within Groups SS}}{\text{Within Groups df}}$

STEP 16: Draw a summary table for the ANOVA as follows:

Source of Variation	df	Sum-of-Squares	Mean Square
Between Groups Within Groups Total			*The mean squares are called S_B and S_W*

Note: At this point, we've finished the ANOVA but we don't know whether the pattern of variances in our scores is a pattern that's likely to have arisen by chance or not. In order to find out, we need to perform an F-Test on our mean squares. Don't worry, it's an uncomplicated calculation!

The F-Test
(F-Ratio)

When to use the F-Test

The F-Test is used when we want to find out if two variances are similar enough to be thought of as having the same source. There are two situations in which this is useful. Firstly, in the present situation, we are wanting to find out if the pattern of variances calculated from our data in the One-Way ANOVA is due to chance or due to our manipulation of the independent variable. Secondly, we sometimes want to be absolutely sure that two samples have the same variance before we use a t-Test.

What the F-Test does

The F-Test simple divides one variance by the other to see how close to 1.00 the ratio is (clearly if the ratio between the variances is 1.00 then they are identical!). The procedure is sometimes called the F-Ratio for obvious reasons.

Calculating the F-Test

STEP 1: Divide the Between Groups Mean Square by the Within Groups Mean Square:

$$F = \frac{\text{Between Groups Mean Square}}{\text{Within Groups Mean Square}}$$

This the **obtained value** of F

STEP 2: Select a significance level (usually this is 5% or $p \leq 0.05$). *Note: There is no direction to an hypothesis for an F-test, so you don't have to work out whether your hypothesis is one or two-tailed.*

STEP 3: Look up the **critical value** of F in the table on page 109. You will need the critical values of each Mean Square and use them as follows: One mean square will be bigger than the other (it doesn't matter which way round it is). Take the df of the greater mean square and look along the top of the table until you find the column with the same number of df. Then take the df of the lesser mean square and go down the left hand side of the table until you find the row with the same number of df. Where the column and row intersect is the **critical value** you are looking for.

STEP 4: Compare the **obtained** and **critical** values of F. If the **obtained value** is greater than or equal to the **critical value**, then we can reject the null hypothesis that the variances are from the same source. They are significantly different.

Beyond the F-Test

There are more questions we might want to ask of our k-sample data than just whether the sample means are different. We might reasonably want to know what the pattern of differences is. If we find a significant F-Ratio, then it might be worth our while finding out which sample is different from which other sample. (It wouldn't have been worth computing endless pairs of t-tests to find this out since we wouldn't know whether the overall pattern was going to throw up any significant differences.)

If our F-Ratio is significant, then we can use further F-Ratio's to compare our sample means in pairs. This is similar to doing a t-test but much, quicker and easier. For each pair, do the following calculation - as an example we will illustrate comparing Group A and Group B:

$$F = \frac{(XA - XB)^2}{S_W^2(NA + NB) / NA \times NB} \quad \text{[Remember that } S_W \text{ is the Within Mean Square]}$$

This is the **obtained value** of F. Next Look up the Critical Value of F in the table on page 109 using the method described in *STEP 3* above. Now comes a tricky bit, in order to get the **critical value** needed to compare with our **obtained value**, we have to multiply the critical value we've just looked up in the table by (k - 1) where k = the number of groups.

So if there are three groups, we would multiply the table value by (3 - 1) = 2. *Remember also that you will have to select a significance level.*

The null hypothesis is rejected if the **obtained value** is greater than or equal to the **critical value** just calculated. There will then be a significant difference between the two sample means.
Note: This procedure is 'advanced' and will not be required by everyone using the ANOVA, so we will not follow it through as a worked example. It is, however a useful and quite rigorous technique which has the advantage of being mercifully easy to compute in comparison to the Unrelated t-Test. The worked example will finish at the end of the F-Test for the Mean Squares.

ANOVA Worked Example.
Our data comes from a hypothetical study in which 7 closed client records were selected at random from last years files of three branches of a volunteer counselling service. The number of sessions over which each of the 21 clients were seen was recorded in the table below. The branches are called Branch A, B, and C. We are interested to find out if there is a significant difference between the number of for which clients are seen in each of the three branches.

Our null hypothesis is that there is no difference between the branches and we expect that any small difference will be due to chance. The One-Way ANOVA will answer this question for us.

STEPS 1,2 & 3 Have been performed by writing the scores in the first three columns as labelled in the table below, and the squares of the scores in the last three columns as labelled in the table below.

Group A X	Group B	Group C X	Group A squared X^2	Group B squared	Group C X^2
10	10	14	100	100	196
18	17	4	324	289	16
16	15	13	256	225	169
9	18	4	81	324	16
6	13	7	36	169	49
11	17	12	121	289	144
12	18	16	144	324	36

ΣXA=82 ΣXB=108 ΣXC=60 ΣXA^2=1062 ΣXB^2=1720 ΣXC^2=626

ΣX=250 ΣX^2=3408

XA=11.71   XB=15.43   XC=8.57

X$_{tot}$=11.90   N = NA + NB + NC = 21

STEP 4:Work out ΣXA by adding up the scores in column 1(see table above). Work out ΣXB and ΣXC by adding up the scores in columns 2 and 3 respectively.

STEP 5: Work out ΣXA^2 by adding up the squared scores in column 4 (see table above). Work out ΣXB^2 and ΣXC^2 by adding up the squared scores in columns 5 and 6 respectively.

STEP 6: Work out ΣX by adding up the column totals at the bottom of columns 1, 2 and 3:

ΣX = ΣXA + ΣXB + ΣXC

ΣX = 82 + 108 + 60 = 250

STEP 7: Work out ΣX^2 by adding up the totals of the squares scores at the bottom of columns 4, 5 and 6:

ΣX^2 = ΣXA^2 + ΣXB^2 + ΣXC^2

ΣX^2 = 1062 + 1720 + 626 = 3048

STEP 8: Work out the mean of each group of scores by dividing the totals obtained in STEP 4 and dividing by the number of scores in each group NA, NB, and NC:

Example $\overline{XA} = \dfrac{\Sigma XA}{NA} = \dfrac{82}{7} = 11.71$

Work out $\overline{XB}$ and $\overline{XC}$ in the same way, see table above.

STEP 9: Work out the mean of all of the scores in all of the groups by adding together the mean of each group and dividing by the number of groups (the number of groups is referred to as 'k'):

$$X_T = \dfrac{\overline{XA} + \overline{XB} + \overline{XC}}{k}$$

$$X_T = \dfrac{11.71 + 15.43 + 8.57}{21} = 11.90$$

STEP 10 : Work out the **Total Sum-of-Squares** by substituting some of the figures calculated above in the following equation:

$$SS_T = \Sigma X^2 - \dfrac{(\Sigma X)^2}{N}$$

$SS_T = 3408 - \dfrac{250^2}{21} = 3408 - \dfrac{62500}{21} = 3408 - 2976.2 = 431.8$

STEP 11: Work out the **Between Sum-of-Squares** by substituting more of the figures calculated above (bottom of table on page 98) in the following equation:

$$SS_B = \left(\dfrac{(\Sigma XA)^2}{NA} + \dfrac{(\Sigma XB)^2}{NB} + \dfrac{(\Sigma XC)^2}{NC} \right) - \dfrac{(\Sigma X)^2}{N}$$

$SS_B = \dfrac{82^2}{7} + \dfrac{108^2}{7} + \dfrac{60^2}{7} - \dfrac{250^2}{21} = \dfrac{6724}{7} + \dfrac{11664}{7} + \dfrac{3600}{7} - \dfrac{62500}{21}$

$$SS_B = 960.6 + 1666.3 + 514.3 - 2976.2 = 165.0$$

STEP 12: Calculate the **Within Sum-of Squares** by finding the sum-of squares for each group as follows:

Example for group A: $SS_A = \Sigma XA^2 - \dfrac{(\Sigma XA)^2}{NA}$

$$SS_{GA} = 1062 - \frac{82^2}{7} = 1062 - 960.6 = 101.4$$

Follow the same procedure for each group.

$$SS_{GB} = 1720 - 1666.3 = 53.7$$
$$SS_{GC} = 626 - 514.3 = 111.7$$

Then add the SS's for each group together to get the Within Sum-of-Squares.

$$SS_W = SS_{GA} + SS_{GB} + SS_{GC} = 101.4 + 53.7 + 111.7 = 266.8$$

Now we can perform our computational check by seeing if the calculated Within Sum-of-Squares is the same as $SS_T - SS_B$

$$SS_W = SS_T - SS_B = 431.8 - 165 = 266.8$$

After a sigh of relief, we can go on to calculate our degrees of freedom, select the significance level and draw our summary table.

STEP 14: Work out the degrees of freedom for the three Sums-of-Squares as follows:
df for Total SS = total number of scores minus 1 = N - 1 = 21 - 1 = 20
df for Between SS = number of groups minus 1 = k - 1 = 3 - 1 = 2
df for Within SS = [number of scores in group A minus 1 added to the number of scores in group B minus 1 added to the number of scores in group C minus 1] = (NA - 1) + (NB - 1) + (NC - 1)
= (7 - 1) + (7 - 1) + (7 - 1) = 6 + 6 + 6 = 18

STEP 15: Calculate the Mean Square values for the source of variance within groups and the source of variance between groups by dividing each of the sums of squares by their respective degrees of freedom:
Between Groups Mean Square = $\dfrac{\text{Between Groups SS}}{\text{Between Groups df}}$

$$= \frac{165}{2} = 82.5$$

Within Groups Mean Square = $\dfrac{\text{Within Groups SS}}{\text{Within Groups df}}$

$$= \frac{266.8}{18} = 14.8$$

STEP 16: Draw a summary table for the ANOVA as follows:

Source of Variation	df	Sum-of-Squares	Mean Square
Between Groups	2	165.0	82.5
Within Groups	18	266.8	14.8
Total	20	431.8	

The F-Test (F-Ratio) Worked Example

STEP 1: To get the obtained value of F, divide the Between Groups Mean Square by the Within Groups Mean Square:

F = Between Groups Mean Square
    Within Groups Mean Square

$F = \dfrac{82.5}{14.5} = 5.689$

STEP 2: Select a significance level (usually this is 5% or $p \le 0.05$).

STEP 3: Look up the **critical value** of F in the table on page 109. We will need the degrees of freedom of each Mean Square and use them as follows: We take the df of the greater mean square (in this case S_B df = 2) and look along the top of the table to the column with 2 at the top. Then we take the df of the lesser mean square (in this case S_W df = 18) and go down the left hand side of the table to the row with 18 at the side. Where the '2' column and '18' row intersect is the critical value 3.55.

STEP 4: Compare the **obtained** and **critical** values of F.
Obtained value of F = 5.689   **Critical value** of F = 3.55

Since the **obtained value** is greater than the **critical value**, we can reject the null hypothesis and accept the alternate hypothesis that there is a difference in the number of sessions for which clients are seen between the three branches of our hypothetical counselling service. If you wish to take your analysis further, see '**Beyond the F-Test**' on page 96 to find out how to test the pattern of differences between the branches.

Table 1   Critical Values of Chi-squared

	Level of significance for a one-tailed test			
	0.05	0.025	0.01	0.005
	Level of significance for a two-tailed test			
df	0.10	0.05	0.02	0.01
1	2.71	3.84	5.41	6.64
2	4.60	5.99	7.82	9.21
3	6.25	7.82	9.84	11.34
4	7.78	9.49	11.67	13.28
5	9.24	11.07	13.39	15.09
6	10.64	12.59	15.03	16.81
7	12.02	14.07	16.62	18.48
8	13.36	15.51	18.17	20.09
9	14.68	16.92	19.68	21.67
10	15.99	18.31	21.16	23.21
11	17.28	19.68	22.62	24.72
12	18.55	21.03	24.05	26.22
13	19.81	22.36	25.47	27.69
14	21.06	23.68	26.87	29.14
15	22.31	25.00	28.26	30.58
16	23.54	26.30	29.63	32.00
17	24.77	27.59	31.00	33.41
18	25.99	28.87	32.35	34.80
19	27.20	30.14	33.69	36.19
20	28.41	31.41	35.02	37.57
21	29.62	32.67	36.34	38.93
22	30.81	33.92	37.66	40.29
23	32.01	35.17	38.97	41.64
24	33.20	36.42	40.27	42.98
25	34.38	37.65	41.57	44.31

Calculated value of chi squared must **equal** or **exceed** the table (critical) value for significance at the level shown.

Source: Abridged from Fisher and Yates, *Statistical Tables for Biological, Agricultural and Medical Research*, Longman Group UK Ltd. 1974.

Table 2 Critical Values in the Mann-Whitney U Test (two-tailed test)

N_2 = larger sample size
N_1 = smaller sample size

0.05 significance level (N_1)

$N_2 \backslash N_1$	2	3	4	5	6	7	8	9	10	11	12	13	14	15	16	17	18	19	20
2	-	-	-	-	-	-	0	0	0	0	1	1	1	1	1	2	2	2	2
3	-	-	-	0	1	1	2	2	3	3	4	4	5	5	6	6	7	7	8
4	-	-	0	1	2	3	4	4	5	6	7	8	9	10	11	11	12	13	14
5	-	0	1	2	3	5	6	7	8	9	11	12	13	14	15	17	18	19	20
6	-	1	2	3	5	6	8	10	11	13	14	16	17	19	21	22	24	25	27
7	-	1	3	5	6	8	10	12	14	16	18	20	22	24	26	28	30	32	34
8	0	2	4	6	8	10	13	15	17	19	22	24	26	29	31	34	36	38	41
9	0	2	4	7	10	12	15	17	20	23	26	28	31	34	37	39	42	45	48
10	0	3	5	8	11	14	17	20	23	26	29	33	36	39	42	45	48	52	55
11	0	3	6	9	13	16	19	23	26	30	33	37	40	44	47	51	55	58	62
12	1	4	7	11	14	18	22	26	29	33	37	41	45	49	53	57	61	65	69
13	1	4	8	12	16	20	24	28	33	37	41	45	50	54	59	63	67	72	76
14	1	5	9	13	17	22	26	31	36	40	45	50	55	59	64	69	74	78	83
15	1	5	10	14	19	24	29	34	39	44	49	54	59	64	70	75	80	85	90
16	1	6	11	15	21	26	31	37	42	47	53	59	64	70	75	81	86	92	98
17	2	6	11	17	22	28	34	39	45	51	57	63	69	75	81	87	93	99	105
18	2	7	12	18	24	30	36	42	48	55	61	67	74	80	86	93	99	106	112
19	2	7	13	19	25	32	38	45	52	58	65	72	78	85	92	99	106	113	119
20	2	8	14	20	27	34	41	48	55	62	69	76	83	90	98	105	112	119	127

N_1: 2 3 4 5 6 7 8 9 10 11 12 13 14 15 16 17 18 19 20

0.01

Calculated U must be **equal to** or **less than** the table (critical) value for the significance level shown.

For a one-tailed test, probabilities shown are halved.

Source : Abridged from H.R. Neave, *Statistical Tables*, George Allen and Unwin, London 1978.

Table 3 Critical Values of *t*

Degrees of freedom	Level of significance for a one-tailed test			
	0.05	0.025	0.01	0.005
	Level of significance for a two-tailed test			
	0.10	0.05	0.02	0.01
1	6.134	12.706	31.821	63.657
2	2.920	4.303	6.965	9.925
3	2.353	3.182	4.541	5.841
4	2.132	2.776	3.747	4.604
5	2.015	2.571	3.365	4.032
6	1.943	2.447	3.143	3.707
7	1.895	2.365	2.998	3.499
8	1.860	2.306	2.896	3.355
9	1.833	2.262	2.821	3.250
10	1.812	2.228	2.764	3.169
11	1.796	2.201	2.718	3.106
12	1.782	2.179	2.681	3.055
13	1.771	2.160	2.650	3.012
14	1.761	2.145	2.624	2.977
15	1.753	2.131	2.602	2.947
16	1.746	2.120	2.583	2.921
17	1.740	2.110	2.567	2.898
18	1.734	2.101	2.552	2.878
19	1.729	2.093	2.539	2.861
20	1.725	2.086	2.528	2.845
21	1.721	2.080	2.518	2.831
22	1.717	2.074	2.508	2.819
23	1.714	2.069	2.500	2.807
24	1.711	2.064	2.492	2.797
25	1.708	2.060	2.485	2.787
∞	1.645	1.960	2.326	2.576

Calculated *t* must **equal** or **exceed** the table (critical) value for significance at the level shown.

Source: Abridged from Fisher and Yates, *Statistical Tables for Biological, Agricultural and Medical Research*, Longman Group UK Ltd. 1974

Table 4 Critical Values of x in the Binomial Sign Test

| N | Level of significance for one-tailed test | | | |
	0.05	0.025	0.01	0.005
	Level of significance for two-tailed test			
	0.10	0.05	0.02	0.01
5	0	-	-	-
6	0	0	-	-
7	0	0	0	-
8	1	0	0	0
9	1	1	0	0
10	1	1	0	0
11	2	1	1	0
12	2	2	1	1
13	3	2	1	1
14	3	2	2	1
15	3	3	2	2
16	4	3	2	2
17	4	4	3	2
18	5	4	3	3
19	5	4	4	3
20	5	5	4	3

Calculated S must be **equal to** or **less than** the table (critical) value for significance at the level shown.

Source: F.Clegg, *Simple Statistics*, Cambridge University Press, 1982. With kind permission of the author.

Table 5 Critical Values of T in the Wilcoxon Signed Ranks test

Sample size (N)	Level of significance for a one-tailed test		
	0.05	0.025	0.01
	Level of significance for a two-tailed test		
	0.1	0.05	0.02
5	0		
6	2	0	
7	3	2	0
8	5	3	1
9	8	5	3
10	11	8	5
11	13	10	7
12	17	13	9
13	21	17	12
14	25	21	15
15	30	25	19
16	35	29	23
17	41	34	27
18	47	40	32
19	53	46	37
20	60	52	43
21	67	58	49
22	75	65	55
23	83	73	62
24	91	81	69
25	100	89	76

Calculated T must be **equal to** or **less than** the table (critical) value for significance at the level shown.
Source: Abridged from R. Meddis, *Statistical Handbook for Non-Statisticians*, McGraw-Hill, London 1975.

Table 6 Critical Values of Spearman's r

N	Level of significance for a two-tailed test			
	0.10	0.05	0.02	0.01
	Level of significance for a one-tailed test			
	0.05	0.025	0.01	0.005
4	1.000			
5	0.900	1.000	1.000	
6	0.829	0.886	0.943	1.000
7	0.714	0.786	0.893	0.929
8	0.643	0.738	0.833	0.881
9	0.600	0.700	0.783	0.833
10	0.564	0.648	0.745	0.794
11	0.536	0.618	0.709	0.755
12	0.503	0.587	0.671	0.727
13	0.484	0.560	0.648	0.703
14	0.464	0.538	0.622	0.675
15	0.443	0.521	0.604	0.654
16	0.429	0.503	0.582	0.635
17	0.414	0.485	0.566	0.615
18	0.401	0.472	0.550	0.600
19	0.391	0.460	0.535	0.584
20	0.380	0.447	0.520	0.570
21	0.370	0.435	0.508	0.556
22	0.361	0.425	0.496	0.544
23	0.353	0.415	0.486	0.532
24	0.344	0.406	0.476	0.521
25	0.337	0.398	0.466	0.511
26	0.331	0.390	0.457	0.501
27	0.324	0.382	0.448	0.491
28	0.317	0.375	0.440	0.483
29	0.312	0.368	0.433	0.475
30	0.306	0.362	0.425	0.467

For N > 30, the significance of r can be tested by using the formula:

$$t = r \sqrt{\frac{N-2}{1-r^2}} \qquad df = N - 2$$

and checking the value of t in Table 3.

Calculated r must **equal** or exceed the table (critical) value for significance at the level shown.

Source: J.H.Zar, Significance testing of the Spearman Rank Correlation Coefficient, *Journal of the American Statistical Association*, 67, 578-80.

Table 7 Critical Value of Pearson's r

	Level of significance for a one-tailed test		
	0.05	0.025	0.005
df (N - 2)	Level of significance for a two-tailed test		
	0.10	0.05	0.01
2	0.9000	0.9500	0.9900
3	0.805	0.878	0.9587
4	0.729	0.811	0.9172
5	0.669	0.754	0.875
6	0.621	0.707	0.834
7	0.582	0.666	0.798
8	0.549	0.632	0.765
9	0.521	0.602	0.735
10	0.497	0.576	0.708
11	0.476	0.553	0.684
12	0.475	0.532	0.661
13	0.441	0.514	0.641
14	0.426	0.497	0.623
15	0.412	0.482	0.606
16	0.400	0.468	0.590
17	0.389	0.456	0.575
18	0.378	0.444	0.561
19	0.369	0.433	0.549
20	0.360	0.423	0.537
25	0.323	0.381	0.487
30	0.296	0.349	0.449
35	0.275	0.325	0.418
40	0.257	0.304	0.393
45	0.243	0.288	0.372
50	0.231	0.273	0.354

Calculated r must **equal** or **exceed** the table (critical) value for significance at the level shown.

Source : Abridged from F.C. Powell, *Cambridge Mathematical and Statistical Tables*, Cambridge University Press, 1976.

Table 8 Points for the distribution of F Levels of significance 0.05 and 0.01

f_1 Degrees of Freedom (for Greater Mean Square)

f_2	1	2	3	4	5	6	7	8	9	10	11	12	14	16	20	24	30
1	161 **4,052**	200 **4,999**	216 **5,403**	225 **5,625**	230 **5,764**	234 **5,859**	237 **5,928**	239 **5,981**	241 **6,022**	242 **6,056**	243 **6,082**	244 **6,106**	245 **6,142**	246 **6,169**	248 **6,208**	249 **6,234**	250 **6,258**
2	18.51 **98.49**	19.00 **99.00**	19.16 **99.17**	19.25 **99.25**	19.30 **99.30**	19.33 **99.33**	19.36 **99.34**	19.37 **99.36**	19.38 **99.38**	19.39 **99.40**	19.40 **99.41**	19.41 **99.42**	19.42 **99.43**	19.43 **99.44**	19.44 **99.45**	19.45 **99.46**	19.46 **99.47**
3	10.13 **34.12**	9.55 **30.82**	9.28 **29.46**	9.12 **28.71**	9.01 **28.24**	8.94 **27.91**	8.88 **29.67**	8.84 **27.49**	8.81 **27.34**	8.78 **27.23**	8.76 **27.13**	8.74 **27.05**	8.71 **26.92**	8.69 **26.83**	8.66 **26.69**	8.64 **26.60**	8.62 **26.50**
4	7.71 **21.20**	6.94 **18.00**	6.59 **16.69**	6.39 **15.98**	6.26 **15.52**	6.16 **15.21**	6.09 **14.98**	6.04 **14.80**	6.00 **14.66**	5.96 **14.54**	5.93 **14.45**	5.91 **14.37**	5.87 **14.24**	5.84 **14.15**	5.80 **14.02**	5.77 **13.93**	5.74 **13.83**
5	6.61 **16.26**	5.79 **13.27**	5.41 **12.06**	5.19 **11.39**	5.05 **10.97**	4.95 **10.67**	4.88 **10.45**	4.82 **10.27**	4.78 **10.15**	4.74 **10.05**	4.70 **9.96**	4.68 **9.89**	4.64 **9.77**	4.60 **9.68**	4.56 **9.55**	4.53 **9.47**	4.50 **9.38**
6	5.99 **13.74**	5.14 **10.92**	4.76 **9.78**	4.53 **9.15**	4.39 **8.75**	4.28 **8.47**	4.21 **8.26**	4.15 **8.10**	4.10 **7.98**	4.06 **7.87**	4.03 **7.79**	4.00 **7.72**	3.96 **7.60**	3.92 **7.52**	3.87 **7.39**	3.84 **7.31**	3.81 **7.23**
7	5.59 **12.25**	4.74 **9.55**	4.35 **8.45**	4.12 **7.85**	3.97 **7.46**	3.87 **7.19**	3.79 **7.00**	3.73 **6.84**	3.68 **6.71**	3.63 **6.62**	3.60 **6.54**	3.57 **6.47**	3.52 **6.35**	3.49 **6.27**	3.44 **6.15**	3.41 **6.07**	3.38 **5.98**
8	5.32 **11.26**	4.46 **8.65**	4.07 **7.59**	3.84 **7.01**	3.69 **6.63**	3.58 **6.37**	3.50 **6.19**	3.44 **6.03**	3.39 **5.91**	3.34 **5.82**	3.31 **5.74**	3.28 **5.67**	3.23 **5.56**	3.20 **5.48**	3.15 **5.36**	3.12 **5.28**	3.08 **5.20**
9	5.12 **10.56**	4.26 **8.02**	3.86 **6.99**	3.63 **6.42**	3.48 **6.06**	3.37 **5.80**	3.29 **5.62**	3.23 **5.47**	3.18 **5.35**	3.13 **5.26**	3.10 **5.18**	3.07 **5.11**	3.02 **5.00**	2.98 **4.92**	2.93 **4.80**	2.90 **4.73**	2.86 **4.64**
10	4.96 **10.04**	4.10 **7.56**	3.71 **6.55**	3.48 **5.99**	3.33 **5.64**	3.22 **5.39**	3.14 **5.21**	3.07 **5.06**	3.02 **4.95**	2.97 **4.85**	2.94 **4.78**	2.91 **4.71**	2.86 **4.60**	2.82 **4.52**	2.77 **4.41**	2.74 **4.33**	2.70 **4.25**

Table 8 Continued

f_2	f_1 Degrees of Freedom (for Greater Mean Square)																
	1	2	3	4	5	6	7	8	9	10	11	12	14	16	20	24	30
11	4.84 **9.65**	3.98 **7.20**	3.59 **6.22**	3.36 **5.67**	3.20 **5.32**	3.09 **5.07**	3.01 **4.88**	2.95 **4.74**	2.90 **4.63**	2.86 **4.54**	2.82 **4.46**	2.79 **4.40**	2.74 **4.29**	2.70 **4.21**	2.65 **4.10**	2.61 **4.02**	2.57 **3.94**
12	4.75 **9.33**	3.88 **6.93**	3.49 **5.95**	3.26 **5.41**	3.11 **5.06**	3.00 **4.82**	2.92 **4.65**	2.85 **4.50**	2.80 **4.39**	2.76 **4.30**	2.72 **4.22**	2.69 **4.16**	2.64 **4.05**	2.60 **3.98**	2.54 **3.86**	2.50 **3.78**	2.46 **3.70**
13	4.67 **9.07**	3.80 **6.70**	3.41 **5.74**	3.18 **5.20**	3.02 **4.86**	2.92 **4.62**	2.84 **4.44**	2.72 **4.30**	2.77 **4.19**	2.63 **4.10**	2.63 **4.02**	2.60 **3.96**	2.55 **3.85**	2.51 **3.78**	2.46 **3.67**	2.42 **3.59**	2.38 **3.51**
14	4.60 **8.86**	3.74 **6.51**	3.34 **5.56**	3.11 **5.03**	2.96 **4.69**	2.85 **4.46**	2.77 **4.28**	2.70 **4.14**	2.65 **4.03**	2.60 **3.94**	2.56 **3.86**	2.53 **3.80**	2.48 **3.70**	2.44 **3.62**	2.39 **3.51**	2.35 **3.43**	2.31 **3.34**
15	4.54 **8.68**	3.68 **6.36**	3.29 **5.42**	3.06 **4.89**	2.90 **4.56**	2.79 **4.32**	2.70 **4.14**	2.64 **4.00**	2.59 **3.89**	2.55 **3.80**	2.51 **3.73**	2.48 **3.67**	2.43 **3.56**	2.39 **3.48**	2.33 **3.36**	2.29 **3.29**	2.25 **3.20**
16	4.49 **8.53**	3.63 **6.23**	3.24 **5.29**	3.01 **4.77**	2.85 **4.44**	2.74 **4.20**	2.66 **4.03**	2.59 **3.89**	2.54 **3.78**	2.49 **3.69**	2.45 **3.61**	2.42 **3.55**	2.37 **3.45**	2.33 **3.37**	2.28 **3.25**	2.24 **3.18**	2.20 **3.10**
17	4.45 **8.40**	3.59 **6.11**	3.20 **5.18**	2.96 **4.67**	2.81 **4.34**	2.70 **4.10**	2.62 **3.93**	2.55 **3.79**	2.50 **3.68**	2.45 **3.59**	2.41 **3.52**	2.38 **3.45**	2.33 **3.35**	2.29 **3.27**	2.23 **3.16**	2.19 **3.08**	2.15 **3.00**
18	4.41 **8.28**	3.55 **6.01**	3.16 **5.09**	2.93 **4.58**	2.77 **4.25**	2.66 **4.01**	2.58 **3.85**	2.51 **3.71**	2.46 **3.60**	2.41 **3.51**	2.37 **3.44**	2.34 **3.37**	2.29 **3.27**	2.25 **3.19**	2.19 **3.07**	2.15 **3.00**	2.11 **2.91**
19	4.38 **8.18**	3.52 **5.93**	3.13 **5.01**	2.90 **4.50**	2.74 **4.17**	2.63 **3.94**	2.55 **3.77**	2.48 **3.63**	2.43 **3.52**	2.38 **3.43**	2.34 **3.36**	2.31 **3.30**	2.26 **3.19**	2.21 **3.12**	2.15 **3.00**	2.11 **2.92**	2.07 **2.84**
20	4.35 **8.10**	3.49 **5.85**	3.10 **4.94**	2.87 **4.43**	2.71 **4.10**	2.60 **3.87**	2.52 **3.71**	2.45 **3.56**	2.40 **3.45**	2.35 **3.37**	2.31 **3.30**	2.28 **3.23**	2.23 **3.13**	2.18 **3.05**	2.12 **2.94**	2.08 **2.86**	2.04 **2.77**

Table 8 Continued

f_2								f_1 Degrees of Freedom (for Greater Mean Square)									
	1	2	3	4	5	6	7	8	9	10	11	12	14	16	20	24	30
21	4.32 **8.02**	3.47 **5.78**	3.07 **4.87**	2.84 **4.37**	2.68 **4.04**	2.57 **3.81**	2.49 **3.65**	2.42 **3.51**	2.37 **3.40**	2.32 **3.31**	2.28 **3.24**	2.25 **3.17**	2.20 **3.07**	2.15 **2.99**	2.09 **2.88**	2.05 **2.80**	2.00 **2.72**
22	4.30 **7.94**	3.44 **5.72**	3.05 **4.82**	2.82 **4.31**	2.66 **3.99**	2.55 **3.76**	2.47 **3.59**	2.40 **3.45**	2.35 **3.35**	2.30 **3.26**	2.26 **3.18**	2.23 **3.12**	2.18 **3.02**	2.13 **2.94**	2.07 **2.83**	2.03 **2.75**	1.98 **2.67**
23	4.28 **7.88**	3.42 **5.66**	3.03 **4.76**	2.80 **4.26**	2.64 **3.94**	2.53 **3.71**	2.45 **3.54**	2.38 **3.41**	2.32 **3.30**	2.28 **3.21**	2.24 **3.14**	2.20 **3.07**	2.14 **2.97**	2.10 **2.89**	2.04 **2.78**	2.00 **2.70**	1.96 **2.62**
24	4.26 **7.82**	3.40 **5.61**	3.01 **4.72**	2.78 **4.22**	2.62 **3.90**	2.51 **3.67**	2.43 **3.50**	2.36 **3.36**	2.30 **3.25**	2.26 **3.17**	2.22 **3.09**	2.18 **3.03**	2.13 **2.93**	2.09 **2.85**	2.02 **2.74**	1.98 **2.66**	1.94 **2.58**
25	4.24 **7.77**	3.38 **5.57**	2.99 **4.68**	2.76 **4.18**	2.60 **3.86**	2.49 **3.63**	2.41 **3.46**	2.34 **3.32**	2.28 **3.21**	2.24 **3.13**	2.20 **3.05**	2.16 **2.99**	2.11 **2.89**	2.06 **2.81**	2.00 **2.70**	1.96 **2.62**	1.92 **2.54**
26	4.22 **7.72**	3.37 **5.53**	2.98 **4.64**	2.74 **4.14**	2.59 **3.82**	2.47 **3.59**	2.39 **3.42**	2.32 **3.29**	2.27 **3.17**	2.22 **3.09**	2.18 **3.02**	2.15 **2.96**	2.10 **2.86**	2.05 **2.77**	1.99 **2.66**	1.95 **2.58**	1.90 **2.50**
27	4.21 **7.68**	3.35 **5.49**	2.96 **4.60**	2.73 **4.11**	2.57 **3.79**	2.46 **3.56**	2.37 **3.39**	2.30 **3.26**	2.25 **3.14**	2.20 **3.06**	2.16 **2.98**	2.13 **2.93**	2.08 **2.83**	2.03 **2.74**	1.97 **2.63**	1.93 **2.55**	1.88 **2.47**
28	4.20 **7.64**	3.34 **5.45**	2.95 **4.57**	2.71 **4.07**	2.56 **3.76**	2.44 **3.53**	2.36 **3.36**	2.29 **3.23**	2.24 **3.11**	2.19 **3.03**	2.15 **2.95**	2.12 **2.90**	2.06 **2.80**	2.02 **2.71**	1.96 **2.60**	1.91 **2.52**	1.87 **2.44**
29	4.18 **7.60**	3.33 **5.42**	2.93 **4.54**	2.70 **4.04**	2.54 **3.73**	2.43 **3.50**	2.35 **3.33**	2.28 **3.20**	2.22 **3.08**	2.18 **3.00**	2.14 **2.92**	2.10 **2.87**	2.05 **2.77**	2.00 **2.68**	1.94 **2.57**	1.90 **2.49**	1.85 **2.41**
30	4.17 **7.56**	3.32 **5.39**	2.92 **4.51**	2.69 **4.02**	2.53 **3.70**	2.42 **3.47**	2.34 **3.30**	2.27 **3.17**	2.21 **3.06**	2.16 **2.98**	2.12 **2.90**	2.09 **2.84**	2.04 **2.74**	1.99 **2.66**	1.93 **2.55**	1.89 **2.47**	1.84 **2.38**

Table 8   Continued

f_2	1	2	3	4	5	6	7	8	9	10	11	12	14	16	20	24	30
32	4.15 7.50	3.30 5.34	2.90 4.46	2.67 3.97	2.51 3.66	2.40 3.42	2.32 3.25	2.25 3.12	2.19 3.01	2.14 2.94	2.10 2.86	2.07 2.80	2.02 2.70	1.97 2.62	1.91 2.51	1.86 2.42	1.82 2.34
34	4.13 7.44	3.28 5.29	2.88 4.42	2.65 3.93	2.49 3.61	2.38 3.38	2.30 3.21	2.23 3.08	2.17 2.97	2.12 2.89	2.08 2.82	2.05 2.76	2.00 2.66	1.95 2.58	1.89 2.47	1.84 2.38	1.80 2.30
36	4.11 7.39	3.26 5.25	2.86 4.38	2.63 3.89	2.48 3.58	2.36 3.35	2.28 3.18	2.21 3.04	2.15 2.94	2.10 2.86	2.06 2.78	2.03 2.72	1.98 2.62	1.93 2.54	1.87 2.43	1.82 2.35	1.78 2.26
38	4.10 7.35	3.25 5.21	2.85 4.34	2.62 3.86	2.46 3.54	2.35 3.32	2.26 3.15	2.19 3.02	2.14 2.91	2.09 2.82	2.05 2.75	2.02 2.69	1.96 2.59	1.92 2.51	1.85 2.40	1.80 2.32	1.76 2.22
40	4.08 7.31	3.23 5.18	2.84 4.31	2.61 3.83	2.45 3.51	2.34 3.29	2.25 3.12	2.18 2.99	2.12 2.88	2.07 2.80	2.04 2.73	2.00 2.66	1.95 2.56	1.90 2.49	1.84 2.37	1.79 2.29	1.74 2.20
42	4.07 7.27	3.22 5.15	2.83 4.29	2.59 3.80	2.44 3.49	2.32 3.26	2.24 3.10	2.17 2.96	2.11 2.86	2.06 2.77	2.02 2.70	1.99 2.64	1.94 2.54	1.89 2.46	1.82 2.35	1.78 2.26	1.73 2.17
44	4.06 7.24	3.21 5.12	2.82 4.26	2.58 3.78	2.43 3.46	2.31 3.24	2.23 3.07	2.16 2.94	2.10 2.84	2.05 2.75	2.01 2.68	1.98 2.62	1.92 2.52	1.88 2.44	1.81 2.32	1.76 2.24	1.72 2.15
46	4.05 7.21	3.20 5.10	2.81 4.24	2.57 3.76	2.42 3.44	2.30 3.22	2.22 3.05	2.14 2.92	2.09 2.82	2.04 2.73	2.00 2.66	1.97 2.60	1.91 2.50	1.87 2.42	1.80 2.30	1.75 2.22	1.71 2.13
48	4.04 7.19	3.19 5.08	2.80 4.22	2.56 3.74	2.41 3.42	2.30 3.20	2.21 3.04	2.14 2.90	2.08 2.80	2.03 2.71	1.99 2.64	1.96 2.58	1.90 2.48	1.86 2.40	1.79 2.28	1.74 2.20	1.70 2.11
50	4.03 7.17	3.18 5.06	2.79 4.20	2.56 3.72	2.40 3.41	2.29 3.18	2.20 3.02	2.13 2.88	2.07 2.78	2.02 2.70	1.98 2.62	1.95 2.56	1.90 2.46	1.85 2.39	1.78 2.26	1.74 2.18	1.69 2.10

f_1 Degrees of Freedom (for Greater Mean Square)

Calculated F must be **greater than** or **equal to** the table (critical) value for significance at the level shown.

Source : Abridged from G.W. Snedecor, *Statistical Methods*, Ames, Iowa : Iowa State College Press, 1956.

Further Reading

If you wish to pursue the subject of statistics further, or if your sample size or significance level cannot be accomodated by the tables in this book, or if your research moves on to require different tests, we can recommend the following books:

For non-parametric tests, you will probably find all you need in:

Seigel. S. *Nonparametric Statistics for the Behavioural Sciences.* New York: McGraw-Hill, 1956.

For further exploration of parametric statistics including multi-factor ANOVAs, there are many texts to choose from. A good starting point is:

Guilford, J.P., and Fruchter, B. *Fundamental Statistics in Psychology and Education.* New York: McGraw-Hill,

If you need to get to grips with quantitative or qualitative research methods respectively, we recommend the following books:

Sanders, P. and Liptrot, D. *An Incomplete Guide to Basic Research Methods and Data Collection for Counsellors.* PCCS, 1993.

Sanders, P. and Liptrot, D. *An Incomplete Guide to Qualitative Research Methods Counsellors.* PCCS, (in press for September 1994).

References

Hogarth, R.M. *Judgement and Choice: The Psychology of Decision.* Wiley, 1980.

Kahneman, D., Slovic, P. and Tversky, A. (Eds) *Judgement Under Uncertainty: Heuristics and Biases.* Cambridge University Press, 1982.

Kerlinger, F.N. *Foundations of Behavioural Research.* London: Holt, Rinehart and Winston, 1969.

Lovie, S. Biases and Heuristics in Judgement or The Knitting Boys Meet the Green and Blue Cab Company. *Psychology Teaching,* December 1983, 7-14. (Association for the Teaching of Psychology.)

Sanders, P. and Liptrot, D. *An Incomplete Guide to Basic Research Methods and Data Collection for Counsellors.* PCCS, 1993.

Index Main entries in **bold**.